FINANCIAL
Parenting

FINANCIAL *Parenting*

— $ —

Larry Burkett
Rick Osborne

Chariot VICTOR
PUBLISHING
A DIVISION OF COOK COMMUNICATIONS

Victor Books is an imprint of ChariotVictor Publishing
Cook Communications, Colorado Springs, CO 80918
Cook Communications, Paris, Ontario
Kingsway Communications, Eastbourne, England

FINANCIAL PARENTING
© 1996 by Larry Burkett

All rights reserved. No part of this book may be reproduced in any form without written permission from the publisher, except in the case of brief excerpts for review purposes.

Scripture taken from the *Holy Bible, New International Version.* Copyright ® 1973, 1978, 1984 by International Bible Society. Used by permission of Zondervan Publishing House. All rights reserved.

Edited by Adeline Griffith
First printing, 1996
Printed in the United States of America
00 99 98 97 96   5 4 3 2 1

Library of Congress Cataloging-in-Publication Data

Burkett, Larry
        Financial parenting: showing your kids that money matters / Larry
    Burkett, Rick Osborne.
            p.   cm.
        Includes bibliographical references.
        ISBN 0-7814-0305-7
        1. Parents—Finance, Personal. 2. Finance, Personal—Religious
    aspects—Christianity. I. Osborne, Rick. II. Title.
    HG179.B83498 1996
332.024—dc20

                                                        96-9882
                                                        CIP

Printed in the United States of America

CONTENTS

ACKNOWLEDGEMENTS

*O*ne of the most commonly used words in publishing is the word "deadline." Webster's has two definitions for the word. The first is the publisher's term of reference: *a set time limit for completing a piece of work.* The second definition must have been written by an author: *a line around a prison that a prisoner crosses at the risk of being shot.*

This book was no exception, and if it were not for the help of two very dedicated and talented assistants, who spent countless hours going over this manuscript, editing and perfecting it, we (Larry and Rick) would be lying somewhere outside that deadline.

Thank you Adeline Griffith and Christie Bowler for your hard work and support.

We also sincerely thank our families for their gifts of patience and for allowing us time away from them to put this work together.

We love you.

FOREWORD

*I*n God's Word, the importance of children is established: *"People were bringing little children to Jesus to have him touch them, but the disciples rebuked them. When Jesus saw this, he was indignant. He said to them, 'Let the little children come to me, and do not hinder them, for the kingdom of God belongs to such as these. I tell you the truth, anyone who will not receive the kingdom of God like a little child will never enter it.' And he took the children in his arms, put his hands on them and blessed them"* (Mark 10:13-16).

Do you feel intimidated or unsure about how to teach your children about money matters? Books have been written that teach parents how to educate their children concerning ways to save, open a bank account, invest, write checks, balance a bank statement, and so forth.

Financial teacher, author, and nationally syndicated broadcast host Larry Burkett, along with the talented author, publisher, and parenting teacher Rick Osborne, will guide you through practical applications for your children. *"Train a child in the way he should go, and when he is old he will not turn from it"* (Proverbs 22:6). If we are going to teach our children to follow Jesus' example, we must convey God's sovereign grace as well as the importance of seeking God's will in everything.

Practical application of biblical money management is important. *Financial Parenting* goes deeper.

Larry and Rick take you by the hand and guide you through twelve key principles, providing ways for you to pass on to your children the broader life application that God owns everything. We are just managers (stewards), entrusted with God's resources—including our children!

Larry and Rick combine their gifts in teaching and counseling in the areas of finances and parenting skills. You will see the truths of Scripture become real. *Financial Parenting* guides *you* through your children's financial walk and into the presence of God.

More than finances. . .Transforming lives.

L. Allen (Larry Jr.) and Lauree Burkett
(parents of six exceptional children)

INTRODUCTION

inancial Parenting is a book that's long overdue. There has been a need in this country since probably the late 1950s to train children in the area of finances. However, when I began teaching on biblical principles of handling finances in 1973, there were no books available on the biblical principles of handling finances—period! As a result, I concentrated all of my efforts on studying the Bible and developing the materials from God's Word to help families manage their finances properly and be good stewards. I recognized immediately how necessary it is to begin that financial training at an early age.

I think back to my own childhood: At 12 years old I was making a living and thinking pretty much like an adult. In my generation, in the 1950s, that was not unusual for a 12 year old. Simply put, my parents said, "You can have whatever you want, as long as you earn it and you're able to afford it on your own." That was a great motivation for me.

Over the years, I've developed several materials for parents to help teach their children but, in general, they were written to the parents and not to the children. Rick Osborne and I met about two years ago and I was impressed with his ability to teach God's principles to children—not just of handling money but many of the other principles: those of salvation, of prayer, of obedience, and of trust.

As a result of the friendship that developed with Rick, we decided to collaborate on a book that would help parents understand the needs of their children in the area of finances and would lay out a simple, clear-cut pattern for how parents can teach their children in this most vital area. So, basically, Rick gathered most of the materials that I had written that either dealt with this subject, or with the subject of adult finances, and he began to assimilate it into a single book that would be directed to parents—for the express purpose of teaching their children God's principles of handling money.

One of the things I learned a long time ago, both about other people and about myself and my family, is that whatever I could talk somebody into, somebody else might come along behind me and talk them out of it. But then I found that whatever I could share with them from God's Word nobody would ever be able to talk them out of.

As a result of that simple philosophy, I began to see success in my ministry. We began to see people who were getting their finances squared away and getting themselves out of financial bondage, so that they could be free to serve God and not be in spiritual bondage as well. I believe exactly the same principle holds true for our children.

If, as a parent, you are not willing to abide by the biblical principles yourself, then most probably you're going to have very little, if any, success in teaching your children how to live by those principles. So I counsel parents: Get your own finances squared away. At least know where you're going and how you're going to get there, and be sure you're being good stewards. Then begin to teach your children.

But remember two principles: one, you're not actually teaching children, you're teaching future adults things they need to know in order to survive in the society we have created for them. And two, remember if you're just giving them your *opinion*, whatever you can talk them into, eventually some slick-talking person may come along behind you and talk them out of it. That's true about credit in general, the use of credit cards, how they handle their finances, and other issues of life.

However, if you can instill in your children the biblical principles of handling money and you can do it in a manner they will understand, that is God's best for their lives. Of course, most important is that they accept Christ as their Savior and as their authority. Then you'll discover that, over the long run, the principles you instill in your children will be there forever.

God doesn't give us principles that slow us down or cause us to live in poverty. It's actually the reverse. He gives us principles to live by because He knows how He created things to work and He wants us to be blessed. It's people's confused principles that are making a mess of things. We can make our children's future more secure by letting the most important part of their inheritance be godliness—doing things God's way. It's of far greater worth than an inheritance of millions without God's principles—not only spiritually but financially as well.

We don't need to be as concerned about what we and others are teaching our children as we do about what they're learning when no one is overtly teaching them. Children are smart enough to listen and decipher information that is presented to them. It gets tricky, even for us adults, when we don't think we're being taught something and our deciphering mechanisms are turned off.

I trust that this book will be a blessing to many, many people, because I believe it deals with what is perhaps the most vital topic in America today. We suffer from a lack of morality, a lack of ethics, and a lack of discipline in our country—in every area. But no area is more visible and more acute than the area of money.

Money destroys more marriages and more lives than any other single thing, and that's why the apostle Paul wrote, *"The love of money is a root [or the beginning] of all kinds of evil. Some people, eager for money, have wandered from the faith and pierced themselves with many griefs"* (1 Timothy 6:10). And that is absolutely certain.

This book first lays a foundation for teaching by addressing some of the financial issues of the present financial condition. We have to ask ourselves who is really responsible to see that our children have a better future financially. Based on financial principles, budgeting does have spiritually redeeming values. In section four of the book we get to the practical aspect of how to get these principles across to the children. There are some practical tips, suggestions, tools, and activities to make the teaching easier. Then in the Appendix you'll find suggested resources for you and your family.

I pray that you will look at this book carefully, that you will study this book as godly people, approaching it from the perspective that you have a stewardship over your children. Then you will impart the teachings that Rick has espoused so clearly and so eloquently in this book. You will teach these principles to your children so that they will have a blessed and joyful life and not one full of sorrow and anxiety about money.

Half of all new marriages in America today dissolve within the first five years and over 85 percent of all those young couples who are getting divorced say they believe that the number one source of their problems was money. They simply didn't know how to handle their finances properly. They got themselves into deep bondage and, as a result of that, they lost their love and respect for one another and, ultimately, decided to go their separate ways. Perhaps this could have been avoided if God's principles of handling money had been instilled in them while they were young.

I pray that God will use this book to help ensure a better future for your children. God bless you.

Larry Burkett

Laying the Foundation

How on Earth Did We Get Here?

A well-dressed, distinguished businessman in his forties paces back and forth in his opulent office, with one hand in his pants pocket. His other hand is holding the phone as if he's grown tired of the caller or, perhaps, the conversation. He stops and tilts his head back, searching for the words and patience that will help him make his point.

"Son," he says slowly, "just because you have checks in your checkbook doesn't mean you have money in your bank account!"

The picture changes: we see a California-style youth sitting forward, elbows on his knees. He occasionally pushes the hair back out of his face. The way he holds the phone indicates he would prefer to be doing something else. It appears the young man is genuinely trying to understand.

His reply comes, "Okay, Dad. Uh, what are you trying to tell me?"

This scene is from a television commercial for a telephone company. It's a poignant commercial because, unfortunately, so many parents can identify with the dad.

Financial I.Q.
What Do We Know?

What is the financial knowledge of the youth today? To address this question, a nationwide survey was conducted to test the consumer knowledge of high school seniors in the United States. The survey found that our youth are virtually unprepared for the many critical decisions they will need to make after they graduate from school.

The survey was professionally developed by more than a dozen experts from academia, business, government, and the consumer movement, and it covered a broad range of questions. The fifty-two-question, multiple-choice test represents the most detailed examination of the knowledge of high school seniors about consumer issues ever conducted. The questions covered six areas of consumer knowledge.

It tested 428 teenagers in eight major metropolitan areas throughout the country and represents a random sample of the nation's high school seniors: roughly 50 percent of the respondents were female; 72 percent were white, 13 percent were African-American, 10 percent were Hispanic, and the remaining 5 percent were Asian or other.

Respondents varied in family income level and their future plans (college or vocational school). They also varied in their personal spending levels.

The results were summed up by the executive director of the

report when he referred to our high school seniors as "financial illiterates."

The teenagers' average score for the entire test was only 42 percent. They could have scored 25 percent just by guessing! The students didn't score above 50 percent on any of the six subjects. They scored lowest on financial services questions (averaging under 40 percent). What are we teaching or not teaching our children that, at an age when they should be somewhat prepared to begin taking on large financial responsibilities, they don't even have a grasp of the basics? This is the generation we want to hand our current economy over to in hopes they can clean up the mess we've made for ourselves. If we handed the economy over today, we would be giving them a federal debt of some $5.12 trillion. And it's growing.

How much is a trillion? If you had a tightly packed stack of $1,000 bills: $1 million would make a four-inch stack, $1 billion would make a 300-foot stack (the length of a football field), $1 trillion would make a stack 63 miles into the sky. Multiply that by 5.12.

It is probably safe to say, considering the staggering problem and the current financial I.Q. of the soon-to-be custodians of this problem, the future may not be too bright.

Let's focus briefly, not just on how this situation affects our country but on how it affects our children. Financial education, or the lack thereof, is not just a current problem; it is one that has been growing worse over the last several decades. Consider the following statistics.

- Our country currently has a 50 percent divorce rate. The number one cause in as high as 85 percent of these divorces is stated by the couples as being financial.
- At retirement, after a lifetime of work, the average 65-year-old American has a net worth of only $100.

Not teaching our children financial savvy is sending them down a road we've proven leads nowhere. Are we as parents purposely sending our children down this road? No. For the most part we've been, and in many cases are, on the same road ourselves.

The father in the long distance commercial is pictured as being financially fit and informed. Therefore the problem he's facing can be considered a result of his own lack of time spent training his son. But unlike this father, most people in America today have a poor understanding of money and how to handle it wisely.

The average American knows very little about finances and the economy. This includes even basic knowledge, such as how to live on a budget and balance a checkbook. For example, say your checkbook shows a certain amount in the bank at the end of the month. The bank statement, when you receive it, shows a different amount. What do you do? Many people, to reconcile this and "balance" their checkbook, simply write the bank's figure in their checkbook as the new total. That is not the way to balance a checkbook.

In the national survey, adults (who were tested a year earlier with the same questions) scored, on average, only 16 percent higher than the kids. Our lack of financial knowledge gets passed on to our children, often unintentionally. This fosters even greater ignorance and increases our personal and national financial problems. This was not always the case.

In many ways, the present national situation is the result of factors beyond our control and far bigger than our in-home training, or lack thereof. Society has a large role to play.

Changing Times—What Happened?

Americans have not always been financially illiterate. The people of the late 1800s and early 1900s were fairly good at handling money. The question is, what happened to change this? Can we trace changes in our society over the past century and determine how they have brought us to the situation we are in today?

We believe that there are a number of contributing factors and that we can learn from history. But as we look at these factors, let's see if we can identify the biggest, most foundational one.

The Canning-Jars-to-Money-Trees Factor

The America of the late 1800s and early 1900s (pre-1920s) was primarily an agrarian society. Most people were hardworking, frugal farmers. They had no choice but to manage their money well. There was no surplus to fall back on, and, for the most part, nowhere to go for help in case of trouble.

All of a family's basic financial dealings were discussed over the dinner table. They were specific and simple. The children were involved and learned by observation. They knew there was no waste and they learned how to save. They saw the direct correlation between work and eating.

Picture a farmhouse, if you will (a little house on the prairie). Every detail of running the house and of growing, gathering, and even trading food is everyone's business. Whether the harvest was bad or good, everyone, including the children, knows the results. Every effort receives a tangible, direct reward and every necessity or delight required labor to achieve. Living in this farmhouse is a typical family from that period. Let's call our family the Andersons. Mama and Papa Anderson have three children: James, William, and young Betty.

Mama Anderson has a budgeting system made up of large canning jars labeled with *Housing/utilities, Food, Clothing, School, Medical,* and so on. The money for each need goes into its jar.

When there are special needs, extra jars are needed. For instance, when Betty needs a dress for graduation (a few years from now), it will be planned for in advance. A goal will be set and a jar will be labeled *graduation dress.* Mama and Betty will work together to save for the material and pattern for that dress.

Then they will make it together.

Children are naturally curious. They want to be involved and they want to understand what everyone else is doing. So the Anderson children understand the family finances. Money is right there for everyone to see and monitor. Where the money comes from is clear. Where it goes is also clear. There's no mystery to the family finances.

Parents like the Andersons were not necessarily more diligent at teaching their kids about finances than parents are today. It's just that the society of that day and its financial system were like those glass jars—clear to see, very tangible, and easy for the children to get involved in.

Now picture a home today. The Wilsons are, by and large, a typical family. They also have three children: Charity, Ryan, and Tyler. Dad has had a rough time in a job transition and money is tight. The kids don't know this because mom and dad don't want to upset them. Besides, the Wilsons have lived for the last two months on their credit cards. Everything seems fine, so the kids haven't even asked questions. After the kids are in bed, mom and dad discuss their finances and budget.

Mrs. Wilson goes to run a few errands. While she's out she gets the groceries and pays the bills. The kids don't know what she's doing, so they don't see the relationship between paying a bill and having electricity, cable TV, or even food.

Mr. Wilson goes to the bank with the kids and has them wait in the car while he cashes his check. The kids have never seen the check. They're not even sure what dad does when he goes to work. After having a bit of a dispute with the banker about his late mortgage payment, Mr. Wilson walks out to the car. He's greeted by a barrage of requests.

"Let's eat lunch at McDonalds," Ryan begs.

"Dad, I need a new outfit for the school trip," Charity informs him cheerfully.

At this point he blows up and yells, "No! We can't afford it! Do you think money grows on trees?"

The youngest, Tyler, is puzzled. He's not really sure where money grows or where it goes. He rarely sees it and doesn't know what it does—except it buys things.

This societal change from a direct correlation between work, money, and goods, to a less visible relationship between them, has had a great impact. The immediate connection between work and money is gone. The knowledge of former years, gained by simple observation, of the variety of places money must go simply to enable the family to live, is gone.

Unlike the Wilson children, the Anderson children (the first family) almost seemed to pick up financial know-how by osmosis—just by being close to it as the family dealt with it tangibly and openly. That too is gone. We haven't yet responded to these changes by adapting so that our children can see the money going in and out of the jars again. Nothing has replaced the canning jars and the simplicity of family finance except, perhaps, a magical and invisible money tree.

Is restoring the canning jars or helping our kids to see and understand family finances the key to restoring our economic future? It is imperative, but no, it's not the key. Let's examine another factor.

The Hand-Me-Downs-to-Handouts Factor

Thomas Jefferson once wrote, "I place economy among the first and most important virtues and public debt as the greatest of dangers. . . .We must make our choice between economy and liberty, or profusion and servitude. If we can prevent the government from wasting the labors of the people under pretense of caring for them they will be happy."

Let's go back to that little house on the prairie in the early 1900s.

The discussion around the Anderson dinner table is what the kids want to do and/or be when they grow up. The younger son, William, wants to help run the farm. He will work very hard, save the money he makes, and build a house nearby where he can raise a family. The older son, James, wants to be a doctor. He's been saving his money and his parents have promised to help. With that money and the use of the carpentry skills he's already learned from his father, he plans to make it through school. Betty, the youngest, wants to purchase her own sewing machine and be able to design and make her own clothes. She will do this for the family she hopes to have one day. She might even be able to sell what she makes.

They all know they have to work hard, develop their skills, and learn to earn their way in life. In the meantime, they make do with what is available, whether it be home-grown, bartered, or hand-me-down.

Life was simple and good. But things began to change. In the 1920s and 30s, people began making the shift from farming to industry. The process of money management, with its close ties to the land, was inverted. The new generation was different from their parents'.

At first this was a euphoric time: the beginning of industry. New inventions, such as cars and other convenience items, were being mass-produced. They were suddenly available to people in an unprecedented way. Things never before available, some never even thought of before, were now there for the purchasing. Houses could be bought more easily than ever before. The standard of living rose and people lapped it up. Spending hit a high as the nation seemed to be on an unstoppable roll. The 1920s were a heady time.

Then the Great Depression hit! People who had been living better than their parents, by far, were suddenly living in poverty. Out of this came a major change that would have long-term ramifications; the role of government began to shift.

Early political and social leaders of the United States had warned the generations to come never to take government handouts. Thomas Jefferson warned that if the government became the provider it would also become the policy maker.

Presidents from George Washington to Calvin Coolidge warned about the dangers of taking public monies to support private citizens. Congressman Davy Crockett stood on the floor of the House and shouted down those who would have taken American tax dollars to support a Revolutionary War veteran's widow. Instead, he proposed that members of the Congress agree to help her from their own resources but not to rob the public coffers—no matter how just the cause.

President Grover Cleveland forfeited a second term in office rather than sign a bill that would have taken tax dollars to facilitate an orphanage in New York.

These men had a gut-level understanding of something we have forgotten, if we ever knew. They knew, intuitively, what we are just now beginning to prove: once the Treasury is opened to the public, there are no limits to the "needs."

Despite the strong warnings and counsel of many of America's early leaders, the government stepped in. It basically said, "We'll take care of you, don't worry. We'll cover your losses." People began to develop the attitude, "We can have these things. We deserve them." They wanted what they had before the Depression hit.

In 1932 Franklin Roosevelt campaigned under the banner of more government intervention in the economy—a direct contradiction to the warnings of his predecessors. When he was elected he did exactly what he promised; he put the government in charge of the finances of America. As a result, there was a further shift from the self-help mentality to a government-help mentality. The attitude grew that, if worse comes to worst, the government will help you. "They won't let us starve," people believed. "They owe us a certain lifestyle."

The things the government promised at first seemed reasonable: they would keep people from starving, give them minimum wage jobs so they could feed their families, and start a retirement plan for them that was an old age supplement. The supplement was never enough to live on, but if you had nothing else, it would keep food on the table so you wouldn't starve. Social Security had begun.

Gradually this base-level government intervention changed. It moved from being only for the worst case scenarios to being for the average case. If you didn't have something, you were deprived; you deserved better. And the government would ensure you got it. Government handouts or entitlements grew into massive programs.

In his famous inaugural address, President Kennedy said, "Ask not what your country can do for you. . . ." He was reiterating what the earlier statesmen had said. At that time those with their hands in Uncle Sam's pockets numbered only about twenty-two million. In the next decade, that number would swell to almost 160 million.

Lyndon Johnson thrust the federal government into the role of total provider of even the most basic needs: food and shelter.

More and more Americans turned to the government to solve their problems. In spite of all the evidence to the contrary, and the soaring federal debt, Americans naively believed they could trust the government to meet their needs. This has grown until, today, 80 percent of all Americans receive some sort of government handout.

Let's go back to the suburbs and revisit our modern-day family, the Wilsons. Dad has cooled down. Tyler, the youngest, is still try-ing to figure out if there really is such a thing as a money tree. The family is sitting down to a snack in front of the television. The news anchor is presenting an article on how the government's new budget is going to affect the youth and soon-to-be-employed of our society. The prognosis seems to be doom and gloom. The government has thrown some paltry amount at youth programs to train them and create more jobs. Education has received no new monies.

Mr. Wilson shakes his head and says, "It's going to be tough out there for you kids. I don't envy you one bit."

The oldest, Charity, says, "I sure hope they didn't cut that schol-arship program I applied for. I'm not sure what I'm going to study, but my friends and I want to go to college."

Ryan blurts out, "I'm going to be rich. No way I'm going to work some flunky job. You can get more money from the govern-ment just by sitting at home watching television!"

Tyler, the youngest, asks if they can change the channel because his favorite program, "The Simpsons," is coming on.

Today's children have little concept of working for the things they want. They don't see the connection between hard work and getting a career or achieving their goals. It barely even crosses their minds. Government scholarships and handouts are so easily accessible; why shouldn't they get their share? There is little thought about the payments that will have to be made when the loan comes due. For the most part, working, saving, and earning as they go is not a natural part of the conversation.

One of the things we as parents need to examine is not only how much our secular society is affecting *our* attitudes and the way we think but what it's doing to our children. Perhaps, more importantly and more specifically, we need to realize how much society's effect on us is affecting them.

Again, like the canning-jars-to-money-trees factor, the hand-me-downs-to-handouts factor has changed our society and our attitudes completely. Expectations used to be that you worked and made your own way in life; now you can turn to the government. Is this change the main one we need to focus on correcting in our children and society? Is this the one that started the decline in our children's financial I.Q.? Or is there something more fundamental that will help us as parents secure our children's future? Let's examine another factor.

The Who-Knows-How-It-Works Factor

Meanwhile, back on the farm, Papa Anderson is having an after-dinner conversation with Grandpa Anderson. Grandpa is offering to lend his son some money to help make up for a thin crop this year, but the younger Mr. Anderson has ended the subject by politely refusing the loan. Although it's a family affair, Papa recognizes that it's always best to pay as you go. That way you know when you need to start working harder and/or smarter. It also keeps you motivated to keep trusting God. Papa Anderson reminds Grandpa, "That's what you taught me growing up, isn't it?" Some heartfelt laughter is shared.

Yes, that's how it works.

The youngest, Betty, looks up and says, "You can have the money in my bank. That would help!"

Papa Anderson takes the time to thank and praise Betty for her generosity and then explains, "God is taking care of us, dear. You keep saving, though. Pretty soon you'll be able to get that special doll you've been saving for!"

During and after World War II the "rich" mentality of pre-Depression days grew again. Everyone had a job during the war. Most jobs were high-paying because the government was funding them by borrowing.

During the war the government borrowed money from the Americans with surplus. These people funded the government on the understanding that the government would pay it back seven years later. But then the government got into social programs and borrowed more. By supporting a large variety of such programs, the government never got around to paying the money back. Worse, they started programs that encouraged Americans to follow in their footsteps and use debt as the answer to monetary problems.

This new generation grew up with a "handout" mentality. Now the government guaranteed the money for houses, loaned money for college educations, and extended a variety of other loans. The government was promoting a system or solution to a problem that they already had proved didn't work.

The debt mentality of the government was passed on to the average American. A good example was the G.I. Bill. It promoted a big shift from the attitude, "If you can't buy a house, you can't afford it," to "If you can't buy a house, the government will back your loan for it, and now you can afford it."

So many institutions became hooked on credit that the government could no longer back all the loans. Non-government-backed loans sprung up. Nowadays you can get 40-year loans and even 90-year loans. In Japan, three-generation loans are available!

Credit: With this big shift in attitude came the advent of the age of credit, something the people of the very early 1900s did not even think about. Their attitude was that you worked for what you wanted. You earned your money, saved it, and then purchased what you needed. The facts of finances were simple and the temptations few—at least partly because no one would extend credit.

Progressively, debt mentality took a stronger and stronger hold on our society. The banks, government, and merchants searched for more and more ways to extend credit. Getting credit became almost as easy as overspending.

In the 1950s a person could not qualify for and receive a credit card unless he or she made a very healthy annual income. Now credit cards are given to high school students. A 1993 study reported that 32 percent of high-schoolers and 82 percent of college students had at least one credit card. In keeping with the financial I.Q. test we talked about earlier, the same report found that only 40 percent of high school students understand what an annual percentage rate is.

Banks realized they could make money through lending (rather than through production, for example). They got hooked on the money they could earn through interest. They realized they could lend money out at 6 percent interest for a house or 12 percent for a credit card. Naturally, they opted for the credit card.

When they had "mined" the people who could afford credit cards, they went looking for more people and made credit cards even more accessible. They reasoned that the majority of Americans are honest and will pay their bills (which they are and will). Even if the banks had a 5 percent default rate, by raising the interest to 18 percent they could handle that default. So they increased the number of speculative loans. The debt mentality was growing.

In our generation we do not live on earned wealth. We live on assumed wealth. People can literally buy things they cannot afford to own. Credit lets us purchase things we cannot wisely afford so that we can have them now. The problem is, because we're paying interest we end up paying more for our purchases than if we had paid cash.

Americans, on average, pay $7,000 per family unit per year on interest, based on an income of $32,000 per year. Over ten years that's $70,000. If they had taken that money and invested it, its earning power would be $150,000 over ten years. The money they had saved from paying interest could have earned them that much again. Extrapolate this over an entire lifetime and you can see the cost of buying on credit.

However, the interest we are paying is a small concern compared to the greater problem that the *debt mentality* fosters.

Our children are growing up and entering the work force, preparing to take over the nation as a generation and, yet, they don't understand the most basic foundational principle of money—one that is so basic it defines what it is.

Money—A Medium of Exchange: The *Webster's Ninth New Collegiate Dictionary* defines *money* this way: "something generally accepted as a medium of exchange, a measure of value, or a means of payment."

Money is a medium of exchange. This means I exchange $20 worth of goods or services for a $20 bill. Then I take that $20 and purchase other goods and/or services valued at $20. In essence, if I earn $20 an hour and my wife and I go out for a dinner that costs $40 dollars, we have exchanged two hours of my life for a meal at a restaurant. The money is only the means of exchange that helps the system work, because the restaurant owner probably has very little use for two hours of my time.

This sounds basic. It is. However, after grasping this simple system we seem to lose it. We don't understand what this means in real life terms. There are only two ways to change the above equation. One, work harder and/or smarter so that my time becomes worth more than $20 an hour or, two, eat at a less expensive restaurant. Perhaps both.

Today's kids have no concept of this basic principle because of the negative factors we've talked about so far. A complex and often hidden financial system, the government giving handouts and, especially, the credit mentality have caused a dense fog to settle on this most basic concept.

Let's return to the Wilsons again, just as "The Simpsons" television program ends. Dad calls mom out of the room. He lets her know it didn't go well at the bank.

"What about one of those companies that will lend you money on the equity in your home? They don't worry about your credit rating," Mrs. Wilson suggests.

Dad loves it. It seems like just the answer they need. "Good idea!" he says. "You know, we should have enough equity to pay off our current debts and bills *and* be able to take a vacation! That would be fantastic!"

The kids have come down the hall in search of dinner plans. Dad announces, "We're going out for dinner. It's celebration time!" On the way out he asks, "By the way, Charity, is your credit card still over the limit?"

"No, Dad. I borrowed some money from a friend and paid it down a bit."

"Great!" Mr. Wilson says. "You charge dinner and I'll pay you back next week."

Tyler glances back at the house as they leave, trying to see the money tree his dad was talking about earlier. It seems to him that a harvest has taken place.

The who-knows-how-it-works factor shows us how the onset of a credit mentality in our society, on top of the other factors we've discussed, has clouded even the basics of how finances work.

Money is no longer viewed as a means of exchange but an end unto itself. The idea has become, "Get as much of that stuff as you can, any way you can, including through credit. Don't worry about tipping the scales back in your favor. Just keep living for today. After all, that's what the government does!"

No wonder the financial I.Q. of our youth is so low. It's amazing it's as high as it is!

But are all these factors the principle reason for the state we find ourselves in as families and as a nation? Let's look at one more contributing factor.

The Get-Rich-Quick-But-Hurry Factor

Life on the farm is kind of laid back. We join our family from nearly a century ago, relaxing after a hard day's work and a warm, satisfying meal. Grandma and Grandpa Anderson joined the family for dinner and the subject of conversation is wealth and rich people. The kids are very interested. It's as if they're listening to a fanciful bedtime story. They have a lot of questions and they let them fly as they hear about royalty, wealthy land barons, jewels, gold, money, servants, and exotic places.

James, the oldest, jumps into the conversation after a short period of silence. "I wonder what it's like to be rich," he says.

Mama, who has also been quiet during this entire conversation, answers her son's question by getting him to think. "What do you enjoy doing after you finish school and your chores?" she asks.

"You know, Mama. I love to read and do some woodworking."

"Your friend Mark has his own horses. How much time does he have to read or to come over here and do woodworking with you?"

"Are you kidding?" James exclaims. "Sure, Mark's horses are what every other kid around here wants, but he barely has time to put his shoes on in the morning!"

Papa picks up on mama's question. "The Bible lets us know that we shouldn't seek to be rich. For one thing, like Mark's horses, riches come with more responsibilities, not less. People who get rich thinking it will make them happy find out it doesn't. So they try to get more. It becomes a cycle and it never works."

Grandma says, "Possessions and things can be nice, but they aren't what being rich and happy are all about."

Betty has been listening and trying to follow the conversation.

Some of the deeper talk has gone over her head. She has been trying to figure out one thing.

"Papa, are we rich?" she asks.

With a chuckle, papa says, "Yes, honey, we are truly, truly rich."

Today we live in, and are raising our children in, a society that promotes and constantly updates everyone on who is making it big with the get-rich-quick mentality. If we ask young people today how a person becomes successful—what used to be a simple question—the answers should alert us to a problem.

The first thing we will notice is that those who answer will have assumed that the words "rich" and "success" are defined by money—probably lots of it. "The American Dream" originally was a phrase that meant life, liberty, and the pursuit of happiness, as well as freedom of religion, freedom from the oppression of government, and the freedom to build a better future for one's family.

Today, the definition tends to have been reduced to mean that you can get filthy rich if you work the system and are in the right place at the right time with the right idea!

The answers kids give to the above success question reflect what they see focused on by the media. The following are some of the answers to the question, *How does a person become successful?*

- Win the lottery (it's interesting to note that, in a casual survey of students in Christian schools, the third most frequently mentioned way to become rich was to win the lottery).
- Think of a great product idea and sell a million of them.
- Become a rock star.
- Become a famous actor.
- Get into professional sports.
- Get into the stock market.

Few answers would have a lot to do with the traditional ideas of work hard, save your money, invest wisely, manage your money, or even work hard at your own business and grow it slowly and solidly until it's a successful company.

On that last point it is interesting to note that, although our system thrives and survives with entrepreneurs and those who pioneer and work hard in business, our whole education system prepares its adherents to go get a job—until they make it big. Not that getting a job is wrong, but shouldn't we also encourage and train those who have the vision and aptitude to pioneer in business? If we did, a larger percentage of new businesses would succeed.

One other fact about business. Next time you have the TV on, notice how television depicts businesspeople. A person who owns and/or runs a company is usually stereotyped as the high-roller who has money and just wants to take it easy, the power-hungry manipulating people crusher, the crook, or the buffoon who is ignored while his or her employees do the real work and make the real decisions.

I'm not saying it's television's job to educate our kids. It is, however, our job as parents to take notice of what our society is teaching, by default, and alter or supplement our children's diets.

The get-rich-quick-but-hurry factor has played, and is playing, an important and devastating role in the financial "dumbing down" of our society. Because of its influence, in the next chapter we will spend a little more time looking at its growth and the various factors that propagate it.

Where Did the "Get-Rich-Quick" Mentality Come From?

*I*n the last chapter we spoke about the factors that have contributed to our poor understanding of finances. Here we want to spend some more time on the specific societal influences that contribute to and propagate the destructive get-rich-quick mentality.

How did we get to the place as a society that we have a generation of kids growing up with this mentality?

Our grandparents knew they had to earn something before they could have it. No one was going to step up and hand it to them; and, they didn't expect anyone to. They were willing to work hard and make something of their lives by building it themselves. That was the case until the 1930s.

Today, we don't want to save for a new car; we want it now!

Borrowing is the way to get it. It used to be that you bought a cheap home, fixed it up, sold it, took the equity, and moved up in price to another one. Then you put sweat equity into that house, sold it, and bought another one. That way, by the fourth home you would have the one you really wanted. By then you would be older, more settled, have a lot of equity, and could handle the bigger house with its attendant responsibilities. Now young couples buy their ideal home first and run into problems trying to make the payments.

Proverbs talks about this get-rich-quick attitude. We fit every perspective of it. For example, we want something for nothing, and we think we deserve things we haven't earned.

What caused this fundamental shift? Well, the first three factors we discussed, and the effect they've had on our society, have a lot to do with it. The canning-jars-to-money-trees factor tilled the soil. It put our children out of the loop as far as seeing and experiencing firsthand basic financial principles.

The hand-me-downs-to-handouts factor changed our society's way of thinking from "you work, you earn" to "the government will take care of us and we deserve it." That prepared the soil for seeds.

The who-knows-how-it-works factor put us and our children out of touch with the understanding of "money as a means of exchange." The seeds were firmly planted in the ground.

However, it's the get-rich-quick-but-hurry factor's influence in our present-day culture that is watering those seeds and causing the harvest of ignorance we see in today's youth. Let's examine some of the get-rich-quick propagators in our culture that are doing the watering.

PROPAGATOR #1:
Advertising

First we should state that we don't think advertisers, or any of the other cultural elements we will talk about in this section, are subversive or purposefully out to deceive and lead us or our kids astray. The advertisers are just trying to do their job and, for the most part, they don't know that the way they are telling us to run our lives doesn't work. Like everyone else, they're making the same mistakes in their own lives.

Advertising started out with the purpose of communicating the availability and virtues of certain products and/or services. Thus, if we as consumers needed them, we would buy those products as opposed to someone else's.

The message gradually changed from simply communicating product information into trying to convince us that we needed products we'd never even heard of before. Instead of "find a need and fill it," it became "create a need and fill it." People were being informed of problems and needs they had by the suppliers of the products that were, purportedly, the remedy. We, the people, can boast that our great nation has solved some of life's major problems like plaque, gingivitis, ring-around-the-collar, bathroom scum, post-nasal drip, foot fungus, jungle mouth, the blues, and the soggies (caused by sagging, leaking diapers).

We've actually learned to like advertising in our culture. It has become a weird form of entertainment. But advertising doesn't stop there. In recent years it has taken on an approach that is a little less amusing. Consider the message of the following commercial.

A young couple in Europe on their honeymoon drives into the long driveway of a world class luxurious hotel that looks like something out of *Lifestyles of the Rich and Famous*. They look at each other with cautious, excited smiles. One says, "Can we afford to?" The other replies, "Can we afford not to?" In the next scene the two are checking in, using their credit card.

What's the message? Your financial state has nothing to do with whether you purchase something or satisfy your desires. The real point is, "You deserve it! Live for the moment! Besides, you can buy it on credit."

During the holiday season there was an advertisement of a young couple who had no money and could not go home to their family for the holidays. It was their first year away from home. Then they discovered a major credit card's travel special! They could charge their airfare home, buy presents, ship the presents home, and not pay anything until June. June, it was implied, is a *long* way off.

The commercial was selling the philosophy that if you want it you can have it. It doesn't matter that June is going to come around (sooner than later). The whole attitude is to live it up now. Advertising has been instrumental in moving us on from the already destructive "bigger and better" attitude to the "more" attitude. We have to have more. There are no consequences for our actions. We can have anything we want. And we can have it now.

Advertising does not prepare us for the consequences of purchasing now: the ongoing payments, the high interest rates, and what happens if or when we can't make those payments. They certainly do not teach us how to handle our money wisely or in accordance with Scripture.

Some advertisers of furniture and other large ticket items run commercials that tell of a special sale: If you buy now, you won't have to pay anything for over a year!

Why is that working? The commercial isn't attracting people who have the money to buy the costly items being sold. If you had the cash you could find a better deal at a store that didn't have to include the cost of everyone's one-year financing charges in their price. It's appealing to those who cannot afford the products and it works because the people who respond have no idea how finances really work. They have bought into the idea that they can "have it all and have it now." And, just like the growing government debt, it will take care of itself! Won't it?

An unfortunate thing is that debt has become something that isn't real. Everyone has it. No one seems to mind or know how they're going to get out of it. And no one wants to talk about the end of the line until it's too late.

PROPAGATOR #2:
Professional Sports, Hollywood, and Rock Stars

If our children are not being taught the proper solutions to money problems, such as stay out of debt, save, work harder and smarter, stick to a budget, plan ahead, and spend wisely, what are they being taught? What are they being told are the solutions to their money problems? It goes without saying that everyone around our children and our children themselves believe they have a money problem. The problem is perceived as simple: they don't have enough. The solution is, "Get more!"

Well, how do you get more? In order to find that out, our kids look around for examples. The examples they see and which the media promotes are actors, professional sports players, and musicians. More recently this group includes the young people who strike it rich virtually overnight in the computer technology world through the stock market.

Rock Stars: The music industry tells our kids that they can have their money for nothing. It's a joke among adults that a rock star can make a fortune and not be that good a musician—never mind a person who understands finance. But what do our kids hear? "Wow! He solved the problem!"

Our society teaches us that if only we had lots of money we would have no financial problems. The answer to all our needs is more money. This is simply not the case. For example, consider professional athletes. They earn large amounts of money.

According to this societal "truth" they should have no financial problems. In fact, many of them experience the opposite.

Professional Sports: In the past I (Larry) participated in a number of seminars for professional athletes. My workshops on finances were always full, packed with people with lots of questions. Most of them wanted to know how they could save on their taxes. Yet, when asked, not one lived on a budget!

These are predominantly men, 21 to 25 years of age, who have been pampered most of their lives; things were bought for them and given to them all through high school and college, as institutions vied for their attention. When they turned professional they were no longer pampered, but they did have lots of money. They were given no help in handling this wealth. In fact, their financial I.Q. is a testimony to the very societal factors that led them to believe more money would solve all of life's problems.

In our society the financial ignorance is so prevalent that someone can get his or her Ph.D. in Economics and never learn how to balance a checkbook. That person can analyze the trends in the economy but not know how to live on a budget or whether to buy a car on credit or lease. These athletes were no exception.

The athletes' questions showed they wanted to know how they could live in a large house, drive a very nice car, take great vacations (all too expensive for their incomes), and still have money at the end of their careers. They were missing the point. Their lifestyles were impoverishing them.

The bottom line is that these young athletes are shocked to find out that making lots of money is not the solution to money problems. People who make a lot of money and never learn how to handle it simply end up in more debt than the people who have less money. In fact, people making moderate incomes, who operate their finances according to sound biblical principles, will be far richer and more prepared for whatever the future holds.

How do we counteract this attitude? First, our kids need to know that hard (or smart) work is the key to bigger earnings. Second, they need to know that proper money management is the key to wealth, no matter the size of the earnings.

Athletes do work hard to get into professional sports, but our children should be told that even *they* don't get rich quick.

The following are some interesting statistics from the National Basketball Association for would-be sports stars.

- Of high school senior basketball players, 2.7 percent play college basketball.
- Half of these get scholarships.
- Less than three in 100 college seniors play one year of professional ball.
- Most pro-ball players have an average career span of three to four years.
- There are only about 348 regular players in the NBA in any one year.
- Only one in six marriages of professional athletes survive the end of their professional career.
- The divorce rate of professional athletes is five times the national average.

We established earlier that the number one stated reason for marriage problems leading to divorce was financial. Obviously the solution to the money problem is not having more. In fact, feeding a low financial I.Q. more money seems to make problems five times worse.

The unfortunate statistic is that only one in one hundred professional athletes end their lucrative careers with any money to speak of. Some, who got hold of financial truth and started applying it before it was too late, ended up well.

For example: Greg Brezina, an all-pro linebacker for the Atlanta

Falcons, played in the NFL for six years. He was making $150,000 to 200,000 a year. He was an all-pro Most Valuable Player when Atlanta was winning football games in the seventies. Neither his house nor his car were paid for and he had sunk a lot of money into land-related tax shelters with a lot of contingent liabilities: if payments were missed, he would be liable.

Greg's wife, Connie, wanted to get their money under control. Greg became a Christian and, agreeing with Connie, decided to take steps to remedy their situation. They came to a class I (Larry) was giving. Then they went to a financial counselor.

Greg and Connie started to budget and to take positive steps. They stopped all purchases, bought property, and built a moderate home in line with what they could afford. In three years they had the house and cars paid for.

When Greg's career ended, they had money in the bank, owed nothing on their house and cars, and could do whatever they wanted. Greg felt that God was calling them into the ministry. They now teach family communications and have influenced the lives of tens of thousands of families. They could do this because they got off the debt treadmill and established a biblically based financial approach to their money.

Another example is the famous Karim Abdul Jabar. He played longer than anyone in NBA history and likely earned close to $100 million in his career. But when he left the NBA he had nothing and owed a huge tax liability.

Hollywood: How about "Hollyweird"? What are our children being told by this influential segment of our culture? Recently a very popular star with our preteens and teens was asked how he felt about receiving $10 million for his recent movie role. His response? "It's not nearly enough."

Now, this reply could have been a quick, funny reply to a nosy reporter, but we believe it summarized Hollywood's proposed solution to the money problem. It's the same solution that professional sports waves in our kids' faces. The solution is "more." There really is no formula that includes following principles. Just work the system and be in the right place at the right time.

The story is told that several years ago an actor was broke. He drove to a ritzy neighborhood in Beverly Hills, parked his car, wrote himself a check for $10 million, and put a date on it. Coincidentally, when that year came around, he actually signed a contract for $10 million. Now, this may be a testimony to determination and hard work. However, the media plays it up for its coincidence quotient and puts a mystical, almost New Age, twist to it. The kids of our society are all "writing checks to themselves." Perhaps not literally, but they have once again been told that more money is the solution. Having more money has nothing to do with practicing sound financial principles.

PROPAGATOR #3:
Big Ideas and the Magic of the Stock Market

The February 19, 1996 issue of *Time* magazine titled its cover story "How to Get Rich Quick." It invited us, as readers, to meet the get-rich-quick crowd. It reported on relatively young (for this kind of success) entrepreneurs who became incredibly wealthy overnight when their companies were taken by "stock market magic."

The front page photograph was reserved for the youngest of the group, Marc Andreessen, who is the technical genius behind Netscape, a company whose aim is to take a strong hold of the internet software market. Marc is 24 years old. Before Netscape went public he owned a percentage of a company that had never shown a profit. The day after it went public, his stock was valued at $58 million. At the time the article was written, his stock was worth $131 million.

The article is a well-balanced one that tells of the level-headedness of some of these instant millionaires and billionaires. But the reason for the tempering is that there are rules about how much of their stock they can cash in—and when. One thing intriguing about the article is that it reports a shift in society's attitude toward people who get-rich-quick.

Historically, get-rich-quickers were met with public disdain and were usually considered people who got rich unfairly on the backs of other people's efforts. Even in the early 80s there was still some strong public sentiment this way. But now the article reports that we, as a society, applaud these people because today's system rewards everyone. There may be some of that involved. However, the stock market today still operates largely on the same premise that it has for decades. We (Larry and Rick) believe the primary reason for the shift in public opinion is that, for the most part, this is how society thinks a person gets wealthy: They strike it rich! We applaud them because we believe they found a key and successfully opened the lock. Of course the lock, it's believed, opens the door to large dollars. This means the end of financial problems and the beginning of life as it should be.

However, as we've seen, that is simply not the case.

PROPAGATOR #4:
The Lottery Legacy

Perhaps one of the biggest elements not just watering but also fertilizing the get-rich-quick attitude in our society and in our kids is lotteries. Lotteries, although still prevalent, used to be a smaller part of life that, primarily, only those who were disposed to games of chance had anything to do with.

Today, lotteries are part of our everyday life. They now operate in thirty-six states and the District of Columbia. In 1993, approximately $31 billion was spent to purchase lottery tickets—a 20.8 percent increase over 1992.

When a certain lottery's jackpot escalates to an all-new high, everyone talks about it. The news media reports on it and even the most skeptical pick up a ticket "just for the fun of it." Everywhere you look, lotteries are advertised. The advertisers know that the best way to influence you is to tell you something you already believe and then link the resulting agreement to their product.

Advertisers play on, and thereby further promote, the I-deserve-it, buy-on-credit, and get-rich-quick mentalities. One big advertising campaign recently showed a series of people saying they were going to win because "it was their turn" (playing on the I-deserve-it mentality).

The get-rich-quick mentality, the whole rags-to-riches concept, violates God's principle of progression: being faithful in little allows you to be ruler over even more. Also, the book of Proverbs tells us, *"He who trusts in riches will fall, but the righteous will flourish like a green leaf"* (Proverbs 11:28). When we look to winning a lottery as our solution, or even God's solution, we've made the answer "more money." That is the center of the get-rich-quick mentality.

What are our children learning (when we don't think they are learning) from our society and the media age? What ideas, contrary to God's, are being so ingrained in them that it will take major consequences of their actions, later in life, to bring them back to God's principles? It's funny how, when we receive the harvest of bad results from planting seeds contrary to God's principles, we automatically blame it on God. We say, "I'm going through financial difficulties. God must be trying to teach me something." Often what is happening is simply the natural consequences of our actions.

More money is not the answer.

Even as a society we think more money will solve social problems. An increasing number of states are legalizing gambling and opening casinos, ostensibly to get more money for public works projects and education. These casinos, and other gambling establishments, further feed the get-rich-quick mentality: "I can get lots of money without working for it."

Unfortunately, along with casinos comes organized crime and other problems. Police forces have to be increased; crime rates soar; and family problems, including abuse and violence, increase. The very establishments that are supposed to raise money for public works end up costing the cities and states far more in "clean up" than they raise.

Practically every Indian reservation now has a gambling casino. The thought was that if there was more money there would be fewer problems. A woman called me (Larry) during one of my radio programs. She receives $40,000 per month as her share of the casino takings, as does every member! However, the problems in the community are even greater than before. Money didn't solve the problem. It made it worse.

Having the "big bucks" certainly does not guarantee freedom from financial difficulties. In fact, lots of money can lead to even deeper problems. The key is what one does with one's money, whether a lot or a little.

Let's join the Wilsons, our modern family mentioned in the last chapter, at the popular local eatery, where nachos, gourmet hamburgers, and larger-than-life pieces of chocolate-covered-brownie ice cream cake are being heartily consumed. The conversation comes around to money—*real* money.

"You should have stayed in football, Ryan," his dad says

between large scoops of ice cream. "You could be on your way to the top right now."

"Hey! Then we'd all be set with the bucks you'd be making," Charity puts in.

"Dad, you know I'm going to win the lottery," Ryan says. "I've got a system! So why risk life and limb for football?"

"Got your tickets for tonight's big draw?" Mrs. Wilson asks. "This might be a bigger celebration than we had planned."

"Wow! Wouldn't that be great?" Ryan says enthusiastically.

The conversation spins off from there into what each one would do with his or her share of $26 million (the lottery total for that evening's draw). Charity states that her share would get the rock band up and running that she and her friends are starting. Then she'd be making some *real* money.

Now the war was on! Ryan responded with his idea! "Hey, that's play money! If you want to see real money, listen to this. I'm going to be the first one to take a lottery to the Internet. I'll get someone to make the software and I'll sell it to every lottery-hungry government in the world. As soon as I have the contracts signed, I'll take the whole thing public and, bang, I'm a multibillionaire overnight. *That's* real money!"

Tyler, squirming uncomfortably because he ate far too much, is feeling quite lost. He tugs on his dad's sleeve and asks, "Daddy, does regular money grow on trees? Or just real money?"

Everyone laughs as Mr. Wilson says, "Don't worry, son. By the time you're old enough to be concerned, we'll be able to take care of everything for you."

We leave our visionary family as they are all searching for enough money to pay the bill for their meal. Charity's credit card was refused after all. As it turns out, Tyler has been secretly saving some money that his grandmother had given him. He kindly offered it and, fortunately, it was enough to pay the bill.

We have covered quite a few of the factors contributing to our nation's poor financial I.Q. The good news is, if we can see what is happening in our society and in our culture, we can begin to help our children recognize it as well. If we endeavor to operate our lives according to God's principles and wisdom, and teach our children to do the same, we can count on God to take care of us. We will not need to depend on a corrupt system in decay. More importantly though, we can know that training our kids to trust and follow God allows us to rest, confident that no matter what the future holds they'll be in the unchanging, secure hands of their heavenly Father.

Parents' Responsibility to Teach

Who Is Really Responsible?

GOD'S WORD FOR A LONG LIFE

*I*n the parable of the prodigal son (Luke 15:11-21), Jesus told of the state of the lost son's heart by showing what he did with money. As parents we need to teach our children about finances, but we need to do it on a foundation of teaching children God's Word and principles while directing them toward and helping them to develop a relationship with God.

Anything that you can talk your kids into, someone else will be able to talk them out of, so we need to concentrate on building our children's foundation. They need to have it ingrained in them both that the Bible is life's instruction manual and that they need to base their lives on its principles and instructions.

"But as for you, continue in what you have learned and have become convinced of, because you know those from whom you learned it, and

how from infancy you have known the holy Scriptures, which are able to make you wise for salvation through faith in Christ Jesus. All Scripture is God-breathed and is useful for teaching, rebuking, correcting and training in righteousness, so that the man of God may be thoroughly equipped for every good work" (2 Timothy 3:14-17).

God's Word also says, *"Children, obey your parents in the Lord, for this is right. 'Honor your father and mother'—which is the first commandment with a promise—'that it may go well with you and that you may enjoy long life on the earth.' Fathers, do not exasperate your children; instead, bring them up in the training and instruction of the Lord"* (Ephesians 6:1-4).

We as parents are so familiar with the first part of this Scripture because we are acutely aware of the fact that our children are supposed to honor and obey us. As a matter of fact we like to remind them of this verse. We've also begun to assume that there is some kind of disconnected reward involved; it says the kids will have a life that turns out okay if they are obedient to us. We assume God rewards them for making our lives a little easier.

If you look at these verses in context, however, you'll find that Paul was quoting from Deuteronomy 5:16: *"Honor your father and your mother, as the Lord your God has commanded you, so that you may live long and that it may go well with you in the land the Lord your God is giving you."* The only change Paul made was that he changed "the land" (the Promised Land or Canaan) to "the earth," making the verse applicable to the New Testament church. But he did not change the context in which it was given.

"These are the commands, decrees and laws the Lord your God directed me to teach you to observe in the land that you are crossing the Jordan to possess, so that you, your children and their children after them may fear the Lord your God as long as you live by keeping all his decrees and commands that I give you, and so that

you may enjoy long life. Hear, O Israel, and be careful to obey so that it may go well with you and that you may increase greatly in a land flowing with milk and honey, just as the Lord, the God of your fathers, promised you" (Deuteronomy 6:1-3).

This passage more clearly spells out the context. Moses was telling the Israelites that if they followed God and did things His way they would enjoy long life and things would go well for them in the land. Then he said, "You need to teach your children to follow God and obey Him; then things will go well for them as well."

So when Paul quoted these verses in Ephesians he wasn't saying that if children obey their parents they will receive a magical, unrelated reward for making their parents' lives easier. There is no such reward. He said the same thing Moses said, *"Children obey your parents in the Lord."* In other words, when we obey God and live our lives according to His Word and then teach our children to do the same, they receive the same benefits of obedience as we do. Ephesians 6:4 instructs us not to exasperate our children; instead, we're to bring them up in the training and instruction of the Lord.

Exasperating our children can be done in a lot of different ways, but perhaps the greatest way to exasperate children is to require obedience without teaching them God's principles. When we don't, their lives won't work and they won't know why. Your children will be blessed for obeying God, not you, but it is your job to make sure you are bringing them up in the training and instruction of the Lord so that obeying you is obeying God.

This important task was why God chose Abraham. God chose Abraham and Sarah because He needed a set of parents who would train their child to follow God. Look at Genesis 18:18-19. *"Abraham will surely become a great and powerful nation, and all nations on earth will be blessed through him. For I have chosen him, so that he will direct his children and his household after him to keep the way of the Lord by doing what is right and just, so that the Lord will bring about for Abraham what he has promised him."*

IT'S UP TO US

Originally, the only mission field God created was the training and instructing of children. If Adam and Eve hadn't sinned, that would still be the only one. God told the Israelites again and again, *"Teach your children about me."* Whenever they forgot this command everything they had worked for was lost in the next generation.

Probably one of the finest generations of Israelites was the one under Joshua's command. They took the Promised Land. Then they got so busy building a life in the Promised Land that they forgot to build a future for their kids.

"After that whole generation had been gathered to their fathers, another generation grew up, who knew neither the Lord nor what he had done for Israel. Then the Israelites did evil in the eyes of the Lord and served the Baals. They forsook the Lord, the God of their fathers, who had brought them out of Egypt.

"They followed and worshiped various gods of the peoples around them. They provoked the Lord to anger because they forsook him and served Baal and the Ashtoreths. In his anger against Israel the Lord handed them over to raiders who plundered them. He sold them to their enemies all around, whom they were no longer able to resist" (Judges 2:10-14). They began to lose the Promised Land when they didn't teach their children to follow God.

Another thing we would like to point out briefly is that when the Bible talks about training and instructing children to follow God and his principles, 100 percent of the time it is the parents' responsibility. You cannot find in the Bible today's concept of "I'll take them to church on Sunday and that's their spiritual life." It is not the local church's job to teach our children anything. They are there to help us in the process. If we rely on them, the same thing will happen to our children as happens to adults who rely on their Sunday morning visit as the sole means of spiritual development: little or no growth.

Further, it is not the church's, nor the school's, nor the government's responsibility to teach our children what the Bible says about finances. It is parents who have that job. Yet, teaching children that the Bible is our guide and that God's principles are the ones to follow is not in itself enough. We need to add to that the *why* and the *who*.

Statistics show us that today only 30 percent of youth in churches have taken ownership of their faith by the time they graduate from high school. A large evangelical denomination recently reported that if they had been successful at just one evangelical outreach—that of their own children—their denomination would be four times larger than it is today.

A Gallup poll showed that 85 percent of decisions for Christ are made prior to the age of 18. This should be the age that we, as the body of Christ and parents, focus on.

One of the key reasons we sometimes lose our children to our culture is that we don't recognize where we are in history and that what our society is teaching is so different from God's Word. Also, once we recognize it, we sometimes focus on communicating rules and reason, instead of the Ruler.

Rules, Reason, Ruler

Josh McDowell tells a story in his "Right from Wrong" campaign material that paints a picture of how we sometimes focus on teaching our children the rules. Josh's daughter, when asked, had chosen to be honest in reporting what had happened while the teacher was out of the classroom. Josh says, "The next day I took

Kelly out for breakfast and told her she'd done the right thing, in spite of any pressure or harassment she may get from her classmates.

"'Honey,' I then asked, 'why is lying wrong?'

"'Because the Bible says it's wrong,' she answered.

"'Why does the Bible say it's wrong?'

"'Because God commanded it.'

"'Why did God command it?' I asked her.

"'I don't know,' she admitted."

The Bible says that God is love. Everything He does is unselfish and giving. He instructs us to do things a certain way because He wants the best for us. He created everything and He knows how it all works. When He tells us not to lie, He's not just trying to spoil our fun, narrow our options, or give us another way to earn goodness points in His merit book. He's telling us that because lying destroys the trust others have in us.

Destroyed trust results in damaged relationships and reduced opportunities. It also complicates our lives and leads us into deception as a way to keep everything else going. In addition, we end up thinking that others, like ourselves, are lying and deceitful. This destroys in us the possibility of allowing anyone to get close to us.

In contrast, the truth promotes trust, relationship, love, and openness and creates opportunities for us. Yes, we do it because God said so. But doing it "because God said so" is a result of trusting God. Trusting God means you believe He will lead you well and take care of you. "*We love because he first loved us*" (1 JOHN 4:19). Our love and trust for God are a result of His grace and love flowing out to us.

God instructs us to teach children this way: "*Children, obey your parents in the Lord, for this is right. 'Honor your father and mother'—which is the first commandment with a promise— 'that it may go well with you and that you may enjoy long life on the earth.' Fathers, do not exasperate your children; instead, bring them up in the training and instruction of the Lord"* (Ephesians 6:1-4).

God tells kids to honor and obey their parents, but He doesn't stop there. He tells them what the results will be: *"That it may go well with you and that you may enjoy long life on the earth."*

Children think about specific things; God shows us how to teach them about specific things. The Bible doesn't just say, *"Thou shalt not lie."* It explains the results of lying and the benefits of telling the truth: *"A false witness will not go unpunished, and he who pours out lies will perish"* (Proverbs 19:9); *"Truthful lips endure forever, but a lying tongue lasts only a moment"* (Proverbs 12:19). "Because God said so" is no better reason for kids than you as a parent telling them "Because I said so."

Josh McDowell Ministry, in preparation for the "Right from Wrong" campaign, conducted a survey in 1994 through The Barna Research Group. They surveyed 3,795 youth from thirteen denominations. All the respondents were young people involved to some degree in the youth programs of their church. The survey examined four categories: love and sex, marriage and family, faith and religion, attitudes and lifestyles. The following are some of the results.

- Of the youths surveyed, 65 percent were classified as "born again," i.e., they have made a personal commitment to Jesus Christ and believe they will go to heaven when they die.
- Youths' responses are more likely to be affected by their views of truth (e.g., there is such a thing as absolute, objective truth and moral standards) than by whether they are "born again."
- One in eleven youths show that they have a consistent, cohesive belief in absolute truth.
- By age 18, 27 percent of churched youth have experienced

sexual intercourse.

- Twenty percent of these youths believe sexual intercourse outside of marriage is moral.
- Nearly 50 percent believe that love, not marriage, makes sexual intercourse right.
- The median amount of time spent with Dad a week is 17 minutes; with Mom, 37 minutes.
- Home is a place where 62 percent of them feel secure and loved.
- Kids favor divorce by two to one for parents who don't love each other.
- To 85 percent, God is the "all-powerful, all-knowing, perfect Creator of the universe who still rules the world today."
- Forty percent think no one can prove which religion is absolutely true.
- One in five think Christianity is nothing special; it's no more true, correct in its teachings, or central to salvation than any other religion.
- Two in five say lying is sometimes necessary.
- One in six say the measure of right and wrong is if "it works."
- Nearly 50 percent base their choices in moral matters on feelings and emotions.
- Youth who believe in absolute truth are much less likely than their peers to wonder if life is worth living.

The survey showed many more responses. (For more information on this we suggest you read Josh McDowell's book, *Right from Wrong*.) The survey showed that the single most important factor influencing the youths' responses, their thoughts, beliefs, and actions, was their belief, or lack of belief, in absolute truth and moral standards. This single issue had an impact twice as great as a born-again experience!

The children who grow up in church today aren't being taught the basics of right and wrong and why God has given us rules to live our lives by. But God's commandment to kids in Ephesians 6 clearly shows us we need to tell them that doing things God's way gets results.

After your kids are given the opportunity to see how the world's way of doing things is flawed and that following God's principles not only works but is the way to a life that works, we still need to take them one very important step further. Let's look at the story of the rich young ruler.

"A certain ruler asked [Jesus], 'Good teacher, what must I do to inherit eternal life?'

"'Why do you call me good?' Jesus answered. 'No one is good— except God alone. You know the commandments: "Do not commit adultery, do not murder, do not steal, do not give false testimony, honor your father and mother."'

"'All these I have kept since I was a boy,' he said.

"When Jesus heard this, he said to him, 'You still lack one thing. Sell everything you have and give to the poor, and you will have treasure in heaven. Then come, follow me.'

"When he heard this, he became very sad, because he was a man of great wealth. Jesus looked at him and said, 'How hard it is for the rich to enter the kingdom of God!'" (Luke 18:18-24)

First, it is interesting to note that this story appears in three Gospels (it's also in Matthew 19 and Mark 10), and all three times the story is immediately preceded by the story of Jesus blessing the children. Jesus rebukes His disciples for trying to keep children away from Him and says, *"Let the little children come to me, and do not hinder them, for the kingdom of God belongs to such as these."*

Right after this incident, almost as an illustration that makes an even more complete statement, the rich young ruler walks up and asks his question. *"Good teacher, what must I do to inherit eternal life?"* Jesus instructed him to keep the commandments and he replied, *"All these I have kept since I was a boy."*

Here was a Jew who was taught God's laws and principles and had kept them all his life, and following God's principles obviously had worked for him. He had done quite well for himself. But Jesus said, *"You still lack one thing. Sell everything you have and give to the poor, and you will have treasure in heaven. Then come follow me."*

The young man knew God's law and God's principles. He knew how to successfully apply them to his life. He knew intimately the benefits of doing things God's way. He probably could have drawn quite a crowd if he had done seminars on how to grow a successful business. But he knew something was missing or he wouldn't have come and asked for a further key.

When he asked *"What must I do?"*, in essence Jesus said, "You're successfully following the principles but you need to follow the person who made them; you know the Law, but you need to know the one who gave the Law."

God doesn't want us to follow Him just so that our lives will work out better. He wants us to get to know Him and learn to trust Him. We are not recommending that you teach children that following God's laws and principles will guarantee success and happiness by the world's standards. We are saying, however, that God wants us to teach our children that doing things His way is the way things were created to work. Therefore, that is how we have the greatest likelihood of success. But if we stop there with our children we'll end up, at best, with rich young rulers who don't know God and/or His grace.

The next thing we need to teach our kids is the need to get to know and follow the loving God who created them. *"Train a child in the way he should go, and when he is old he will not turn from it"* (Proverbs 22:6). There has been some debate over whether this verse guarantees the salvation of our children if we train them correctly. In order to answer that question let's look at the context.

This verse is found in the book of Proverbs, which is not a book of promises or laws. It's a book of principles. In other words, Proverbs 22:6 is a principle, the likely scenario, the usual cause and effect. It is not a guarantee. To illustrate this: "*Lazy hands make a man poor, but diligent hands bring wealth*" (Proverbs 10:4). Of course, everyone knows a hard worker who is poor and a lazy person who is better off financially. It's not a guarantee. It is a principle that, when applied to our lives with other principles, garners the best case scenario.

We can bring up children in the way they should go, living out God's principles and laws, and these principles will carry them through as they did the rich young ruler. But we need to take our children beyond the rule and even beyond the reason for the rule. We need to take them to the Ruler. Jesus said, **"Let the little children come to me!"** (emphasis added).

How do we make sure as parents that we are teaching our children the rules and the reasons and introducing them to the Ruler when it comes to "financial parenting?"

Financial parenting is the parenting process that recognizes and uses the teaching of biblical financial principles to our children as a basic hands-on tool for communicating and establishing greater spiritual principles.

We teach our kids to obey God with and in their finances, showing them that God's ways and principles work out best for us because God is good and faithful and He loves us. With each financial principle we establish not only the rule but the reason, and with the reason we help them get to know the Ruler. Then we take what is learned and apply the principles to other areas of our children's lives, using what they learned in finances as the example.

The attitude toward finances is an indicator of the heart. Jesus said, *"For where your treasure is, there your heart will be also"* (Matthew 6:21). What was the one thing the rich young ruler lacked? Jesus told him to sell everything and give to the poor. Then he would have what he lacked: treasure in heaven. Jesus says that we can get our hearts in the right place by putting our treasures in the right place.

What we intend to do, in the following chapters, is show you as a parent how to help your children bury their treasures in the right spot. Then you can watch their hearts respond and follow. But, first we must take a short break for "station identification": we as parents should have both our self-expectations and child-expectations tuned to *grace*.

Foundational Principles

What's Money Got To Do With It?

THE (GENEROUS) SHEEP AND THE (GREEDY) GOATS

(Adapted from Matthew 25:31-40)

*W*hen the Son of Man comes in His glory with all the angels He will sit on His throne in heavenly glory. All the nations will be gathered before Him and He will separate the people one from another as a shepherd separates the sheep from the goats. He will put the (generous) sheep on His right and the (greedy) goats on His left.

Then the King will say to those (generous sheep) on His right, *"Come, you who are blessed by my Father; take your inheritance, the kingdom prepared for you since the creation of the world. For I was hungry and you gave me something to eat."* (It was tough, I know, but you gave to that halfway house when you had barely enough for your own family. And you shared your groceries with your brother's family when they fell on hard times.)

"I was thirsty and you gave me something to drink." (Remember that time you were on a family vacation and saw that man pass out from heat and dehydration? You and your family put your vacation on hold for an afternoon while you got some water down his throat and took him to the hospital. You almost passed out from the heat yourself. Your family will never forget it.)

"I was a stranger and you invited me in." (That was classic—the time you taught your kids to be careful how they treat strangers. "It could be an angel," you said. You're still not sure, are you? That lady, Evelyn, was walking down your street in a blizzard. She wasn't dressed well for it, either. The kids still talk about how you had your boots and coat on in less than 30 seconds after your youngest said, "Daddy, that lady fell down." You had her inside in minutes and your wife got her some warm clothes and a blanket while the kids made her hot cocoa. What started out for that lady as car trouble on the wrong night turned into an opportunity for your family to share My love. She's here with Me, waiting to see you.)

"I needed clothes and you clothed me." (Now this one was just one of many you don't know about. You recall the commitment you and your entire family made to give your clothes to the shelter? You always made sure they were clean and in good repair when you dropped them off. Well, I was able to use that. I prompted you to make that commitment just after a woman prayed. She was a single mom with kids, the same boy and girl mix as yours, but one year younger. She asked Me to provide her children with clothing as they grew up. She wept every time she went to the thrift store and the perfect clothing for her and her kids was there. Her entire family and several others are here as a result of that testimony of answered prayer.)

"I was sick and you looked after me." (This one was simple for you but so effective. You gave out of each pay check to the company benevolence fund. It paid the medical bills of anyone in the

company not covered by the medical plan who encountered an emergency. And, of course, that time your uncle was in the hospital for three months: No one else in the family had much to do with him, but you and your family sacrificed to go and visit him twice a week. You know, of course, that he died in the hospital. But you weren't absolutely sure if he prayed the prayer you talked to him about. Yes, he did. He's also here, waiting to see you.)

"I was in prison and you came to visit me." (You remember that man who overheard you and your wife talking about God in the restaurant and came over to introduce himself? You answered his questions, prayed with him, and continued to meet with him while he awaited trial. He wasn't my son when he committed the crime, but he was when you helped him to realize he was valued by Me. You visited him in prison and helped him lead others to Me. He's here too.)

Then the righteous (generous sheep) will answer Him, *"Lord, when did we see you hungry and feed you, or thirsty and give you something to drink? When did we see you a stranger and invite you in, or needing clothes and clothe you? When did we see you sick or in prison and go to visit you?* (None of those people you mentioned were you, were they?)

"The King will reply, 'I tell you the truth, whatever you did for one of the least of these brothers of mine, you did for me.'" (How you have spent and used your resources has demonstrated how you felt about Me.) *"Come, you who are blessed by my Father."* (Oh, you'll be pleased to know that your children, who were with you on these and other occasions, followed your example. They are counted with the sheep too.)

In His teachings and parables—whether the rich young ruler, the lost son, the widow's mite, the sheep and the goats, or many others—Jesus taught that what we do with our money and our possessions is a direct reflection of what is in our hearts. Our checkbooks are like thermometers, measuring the heat of our love and commitment to God and His principles.

WHAT DOES THIS MEAN FOR US?

Does all this nullify the fact that we are saved by faith in God's grace through Christ? No, of course not. However, James did say that faith without works is dead, and those who hear God's Word, ways, and principles, but don't do them, deceive themselves.

If by faith we receive God's grace, we then need to begin demonstrating our faith by growing and changing under God's hand and through the power of His Spirit. The life area Jesus used over and over again as the yardstick to determine how the growth was coming along was that thing called worldly wealth. *Money.*

Jesus said, "*Where your treasure is there will your heart be also*" (Luke 12:34). The sheep and the goats both thought they had a place in God's kingdom. But only the sheep had demonstrated that their treasure was in the right place and, therefore, they really did have a place.

The clear principle is, "How we handle our finances demonstrates our hearts." It is a complete indicator—one that works without exception. Jesus said, "*You cannot serve both God and Money*" (Luke 16:13). You will serve one or the other. Your heart will be devoted to the one you serve, and your actions will demonstrate which you are serving.

If we understand this we have a responsibility. First, our responsibility is to God to demonstrate our faith by what we do with, and how we handle, our finances. We say "how we handle" because charity is not the only way we demonstrate our faith through finances. We also demonstrate our faith in God when we follow His principles for handling other areas of our finances: debt, saving, planning, and so on.

Further, we somehow need to help our children to have their treasures buried in the right place and to serve God, not money. If we allow our children to buy into the world's way of handling finances and what progressive generational thought is currently teaching, they automatically will learn the principles behind those methods. Then those are the principles they will apply to the rest of their lives.

In other words, their hearts will follow where their treasures have been buried. However, if we teach our kids God's way of handling finances, they'll learn God's principles and be able to govern their whole lives according to those principles. When we show them where God wants them to bury their treasures, and how to bury them there, their hearts will follow.

The next question then becomes, "Can we really steer the placement of our children's affections or treasures by teaching them what to do with their money?"

Isn't that what Jesus was doing with the rich young ruler? He didn't tell him to go and change his heart. No, He told him to go, sell everything he had, and give to the poor; then he would have treasure in heaven. In other words, Jesus said that if the rich man did the right thing according to Jesus' words, his heart or the placement of his treasure would follow.

This is why *financial parenting* is so very important! If we can teach our children to follow God's principles in finances it will literally cause their hearts to be focused on God. Of course, we can't just teach how to best follow the rules, like the rich young ruler had been doing. Our teaching must include showing our kids why God's principles work and why He gave them to us. Then we can help them apply these same principles to the other areas of their lives so they will grow in relationship with God.

Our goal is to help our children bury their treasures in the right place and encourage their hearts to follow. Think of it like this: if we go faster in our cars, the speedometer climbs; but if the speedometer is climbing, it's safe to assume we are going faster.

We are not talking about teaching kids primarily about finances but also teaching them about God. We are using the hands-on tool of finances that God shows us how to use. However, the bottom line isn't teaching finances. It's teaching our children about God by teaching them His financial principles. That works.

Children think in tangible terms; they understand physical things and practical analogies. They understand more difficult things only when compared to simpler things. What a great place to start! Money is a tangible object, and the things we do with it can be used in every case to clearly demonstrate greater spiritual principles.

We titled this chapter, "What's Money Got To Do with It?" Money has everything to do with it!

Is Teaching Biblical Financial Principles Really a Parental Responsibility?

*N*ow we will look at nine financial topics and the biblical principles behind them. We'll show how the principles our children learn while they are learning God's way to handle finances will affect every other area of their lives.

STEWARDSHIP

When we put money into our children's hands and begin to teach them the concept of stewardship—that money is a trust given to them by God and that they need to handle it the way the Master directs—we have laid the foundation to teach much, much more. We teach them to follow the Master by learning what the Bible says to do with money and by praying for wisdom and direction in its usage.

Once children have learned to follow God's Word and pray for wisdom and direction in their finances, it's a breeze to use that foundation to take them to the next step.

Jesus is Lord of our entire lives. He wants us to follow His principles and pray for wisdom concerning every area of our lives: behavior, money, character, marriage, career, ministry, and everything else. When we don't teach our children how to handle money according to God's stewardship principle, but we teach, through example and/or negligence, that we can do anything we want with money because it's not really important to God, the effects are far-reaching.

The negative and misleading principles they learn from us—"Do what seems right to you" and "Make your own decisions"—become their foundation. These will be applied naturally to the other areas of their lives. The result? We end up with kids who make life decisions without considering God. When we then try to tell them to follow God's principles in, or pray about, their careers, businesses, or choice of marriage partners, it's easy for them to see this as too lofty a concept.

Our older children probably won't understand why we have to be so "hyper-spiritual." Or they might mentally assent to it because they understand it's the "Christian" thing to do. Yet they will have no practical understanding of how to find God's will and wisdom, because in all smaller things they have made their own decisions. God needs to be the Lord of how our children spend their allowances before we can expect them to make Him Lord of who they will marry!

The Financial Guidebook for Life

When we teach our young children what the Bible says about finances and help them to follow God's principles and see the results, we have established more than financial principles in their lives. Here's an example.

When I (Rick) was 16 years old, I hadn't given my life to Christ yet. My mother had always taught us about tithing, so I understood it was what God wanted me to do. I worked all summer that year and gave 10 percent of my income to a church. At the end of that summer, looking back, I had enjoyed myself immensely. I always seemed to have enough money to supply my needs—and then some. I had even saved enough to buy myself a motorcycle!

The next summer I wasn't really interested in giving anything to the church. I wanted an even better summer than last year, so I kept all my money to myself. At the end of that summer I was astonished. I had worked harder and more hours than the previous year and had received a pay raise over the summer; yet, I always seemed to be broke. I never had enough to do what I wanted to do. At the end of that summer I didn't have even a dollar saved and had purchased nothing of worth.

As a 17 year old, even as a non-Christian, no one had to sit me down and explain what made the difference. More importantly, it wasn't just the idea of tithing that now would stick with me forever. Any other life principle that could be shown to me in the Bible had instant credibility. I believe this helped when I gave my life to Christ a year later. As a result of this lesson, what I learned from God's Word about salvation carried a lot of weight.

Carol, a dentist, tells the story of struggling to make ends meet in her newly established practice. One day when she went out with her dad he asked her point blank if she was tithing. The answer was something to the effect of, "Dad, you're not listening. I can't even pay the bills I have, never mind give anything to the church!"

Her dad then said an amazing thing. After explaining how giving the first part of our income demonstrates to God our trust in

Him, he said, "Tithe for one year. If you can't confidently say at the end of that year that you're better off for tithing and trusting God, I'll personally pay back every cent you gave to the church."

It wasn't the guarantee that motivated or convinced Carol. What impacted her was the strong conviction that enabled her father to make that guarantee. A year later she had become a great advocate of tithing. Her practice not only had turned around but was thriving.

However, the really remarkable change in Carol wasn't in her finances. It was in her passion for learning and following God's principles for her life.

When we teach our children to follow the teaching of the Bible in their finances, we've laid the foundation for God's Word to be life's guidebook. Having built the foundation in a hands-on area like finances, it's easy then to direct them to God's Book with every question life poses. It's also easier, once our children have learned and experienced the working of God's Word, to help them develop a love and passion for reading and studying it.

TITHING AND GIVING

It is perhaps appropriate, after the life examples you have just read, to talk about giving to the local church. When we teach our children to give to the local church, we again lay the groundwork for a tremendously important foundation.

First let's look at the negative side. What do we teach our children about the local church when they don't *see* us give there (whether or not we do)? Or how about when they see us haphazardly give a few dollars here and there, after being emotionally moved by the service or made to feel guilty?

We demonstrate and transfer to them what we obviously believe: The local church is man's idea, it's generally a waste of our good resources, and it really isn't our responsibility. (It's amazing what we show, and thereby teach, when we aren't intending to teach anything.)

The Tithe

Statistics show that less than 34 percent of families attending church regularly give 10 percent or more of their finances to the church. Forty percent give 3 percent or less of their income and 26 percent give virtually nothing. And according to a December 1994 report from Empty Tomb, Inc., the average American spends nearly as much each month on the purchase of alcoholic beverages.[1] These numbers paint a picture of the American church-goer's real attitude toward the church. Unfortunately, they also reflect where we are in our commitment to God and to following His principles.

We would like to pause here for a moment to address all those who are being offended by this topic because you come down on the other side of the tithe debate. In other words, you don't believe tithing is a New Testament principle. We promise we won't go into the usual debate here. However, we do want to give you something to think about.

Arguing over whether tithing is a New Testament concept is missing the point. First of all, 100 percent of everything we have is God's. First Corinthians 10:26 quotes Psalm 24:1 on this point, *"The earth is the Lord's, and everything in it, the world, and all who live in it."* The Bible says, *"Naked I came from my mother's womb, and naked I will depart"* (Job 1:21). If we really owned anything, God would probably let us take it with us.

God has given His things into our care. We are stewards of the Master's possessions. *"But remember the Lord your God, for it is he who gives you the ability to produce wealth"* (Deuteronomy 8:18). (See also Genesis 1:28-30; Psalm 8; Psalm 115:16.)

Most people agree on this point and then get caught up in the "how much?" Originally the tithe was a simple demonstration of man's commitment to God and was given out of reverence and gratitude. Abraham and Jacob tithed long before the Law was given. Later, the tithe was used to pay for the operation of the gathering place for community worship. In the Old Testament this was the tabernacle and, later, the temple.

Tithes, which were often produce rather than money, were given into the storehouse. Out of the storehouse the Levites and priests were provided for. The storehouse contents also were used to care for the needs of traveling teachers and prophets, as well as widows, orphans, and the poor. The responsibility of caring for the place of worship, those who worked there, and the needy (Israelites and Gentiles living among them) belonged to the community of Israel.

Ideally, today the equivalent of the storehouse is the local church. Paul effectively transfers Old Testament obligations into a New Testament context without changing or qualifying a single thing. He quotes liberally from the Old Testament regarding the principles God established for support and payment of workers and leaders. He transfers these Old Testament responsibilities onto New Testament believers.

"For it is written in the Law of Moses: 'Do not muzzle an ox while it is treading out the grain.' Is it about oxen that God is concerned? Surely he says this for us, doesn't he? Yes, this was written for us, because when the plowman plows and the thresher threshes, they ought to do so in the hope of sharing in the harvest. If we have sown spiritual seed among you, is it too much if we reap a material harvest from you? . . . Don't you know that those who work in the temple get their food from the temple, and those who serve at the altar share in what is offered on the altar? In the same way, the Lord has commanded that those who preach the gospel should receive their

living from the gospel" (1 Corinthians 9:9-14).

The early church followed the Old Testament principle of bringing offerings and supplies to care for the needy among them (see Acts 4). In 2 Corinthians, chapters 8 and 9, Paul is dealing with the issue of caring for those in need, especially in the body of Christ. *"Because of the service by which you have proved yourselves, men will praise God for the obedience that accompanies your confession of the gospel of Christ, and for your generosity in sharing with them and with everyone else"* (2 Corinthians 9:13). This caring is our responsibility. Jesus clearly makes the same point in the story of the sheep and goats.

So we see that the responsibilities of following a guideline of 10 percent still exists. Even if we don't believe in the percentage, we must accept the responsibility. Judging by the financial needs of most churches today, due to the lack of individual conviction manifested in regular giving, we probably should be thankful to have 10 percent as a guideline. It's unlikely, once we have seriously taken on the responsibility, that even 100 percent of our individual incomes could meet the need!

The Church

Once they're living on their own, over 70 percent of churched youth stop attending church regularly—for a time or completely. It seems they could be learning their attitudes toward church from the attitudes we demonstrate with our giving. When we teach our kids to tithe we can begin to teach them the importance, biblical requirement, and reasons for church attendance and participation.

What should be our attitude, held and demonstrated to our children, toward the church? Consider this: The whole of the New Testament is consumed with and centered around establishing the New Testament church in and through local churches.

Yet, somehow, many Christians today seem to have the idea

that the local church is something pastors push on us so they can have bigger congregations and get our money. Not so. The local church is God's idea. It is one of the keys to personal, family, and community spiritual growth and to reaching and discipling the world.

The point in all this is that the church is important. If we teach our children through instruction and example to give to the church, it gives us the opportunity to teach them their place and responsibility in the church. It also allows us to teach them about the role of the church and church community in their lives.

In essence, showing them where God wants them to place their money shows them what to treasure and helps to steer their hearts to where God wants them. This is a big step toward changing the statistics and keeping our children in church. Teaching our children to tithe is a starting place. We won't find many committed tithers not attending church. Their hearts follow their treasures.

Missions

We can establish another truth in our children through teaching them to give to missions. (The average North American church-going family spends more money on soft drinks than it does on missions.)

When we get involved in supporting missions we have a foundation that gives us the opportunity to teach our kids that it is our responsibility to reach the lost (see 2 Corinthians 5:18-21).

When we teach our children to give to others who are in need and to share what God has given them, we begin to teach them not to be concerned only with themselves but to look to the needs of others (see Philippians 2:4). They learn others' needs are not only physical but emotional and spiritual as well.

This principle then can be applied to relationships, setting priorities, and many other areas of life in which a tendency toward self can creep in. In this way we establish the foundation to help our kids get their focus off "me" and "mine" and onto loving and helping others. We have the foundation to turn them into the generous sheep of the parable.

Another very important thing our kids can learn from teaching them to give is what we call the *first principle*. Often our reactions, and our children's, to giving to the church, to missions, and to meeting the needs of others is, "Hey, what about *my* needs?"

The first principle is that God is our provider. Our incomes, savings, jobs, investments, and possessions are not our wealth, security, or source of provision. These things may be the way God provides for us, but we are not to set our eyes on them as our means of support.

When we feel ourselves starting to have that inward complaint, the fear for our own provision as we obey God and give, it should be a sign to us to stop and check our hearts to see if our confidence is based in God's ability to care for us.

This confidence is the secret of contentment. Paul says, *"I have learned to be content whatever the circumstances. I know what it is to be in need, and I know what it is to have plenty. I have learned the secret of being content in any and every situation, whether well fed or hungry, whether living in plenty or in want. I can do everything through him who gives me strength"* (Philippians 4:11-13).

Remember the rich young ruler? He did not have this confidence. He had taken his eyes off God as his source and off his relationship with God as being key. He looked at his wealth as his security.

We need to be aware of opportunities to bring this home to our children. We have a wonderful opportunity to establish many great, life-changing principles in our children when we teach them through the hands-on tool of giving. In the teaching of God's financial principles, God really has supplied us with the most amazing user-friendly, hands-on building blocks ever devised for teaching and training our children in the way they should go.

As we go through some more of the foundational building blocks of *financial parenting*, remember the key to this system: learning to recognize the opportunities to teach deeper spiritual truths in everyday, practical training. These opportunities don't just come out of teaching financial principles. They can come from an incident over the last cookie, a disagreement between brother and sister, or even the training of a pet.

But finances is an area that consistently provides us with a great springboard. We say "consistently" because finance is a discipline that touches every area of our lives and requires a consistent focus. No other area provides this kind of teaching opportunity for biblical principles so consistently and with such focus. The application of principles learned in this simple-to-follow-and-understand area can be applied so easily to other areas of our children's lives.

FINANCIAL CONTENTMENT

The foundational Bible principle that can be taught through financial contentment seems obvious. Learning financial contentment would lead to an open door for teaching contentment in every area. Yes! And, although it seems obvious, the crossover and necessity for this is profound.

We talked about the Get-Rich-Quick-But-Hurry Factor and we talked about kids today learning from practically every voice around them that the answer to money problems is more money. Contentment gives our children the artillery with which to fight that onslaught. Contentment is peace that comes from learning to trust God in His timing and the consistent, long-term application of His principles and knowing always that He is on the throne and in control.

The word contentment literally means "to be enough." Paul

said, *"I am not saying this because I am in need, for I have learned to be content whatever the circumstances. I know what it is to be in need, and I know what it is to have plenty. I have learned the secret of being content in any and every situation, whether well fed or hungry, whether living in plenty or in want. I can do everything through him who gives me strength"* (Philippians 4:11-13).

Paul was content even when he was in need. That's because God was his "enough." The secret is that our contentment is to spring from our relationship with and trust in God. *"Keep your lives free from the love of money and be content with what you have, because God has said, 'Never will I leave you; never will I forsake you'"* (Hebrews 13:5).

Contentment in these terms, especially in our culture, can be a lofty ideal to teach and next to impossible to get our children to grasp. But, once again, if we simplify the concept and give it a specific application in the area of finances, it gets easier to teach and to grasp. (Or is that to grasp and to teach and to grasp?)

One of our (Rick's and Elaine's) daughters, Rikki, earned some money when she was 6 years old from being involved in a studio recording. When she received her money, we helped her figure out how much to give to the church, how much to save, and how much she could spend. Once she knew how much she could spend, she got out a special mail order catalog and decided on all the things she wanted to buy. When we showed her that she only had enough for one of the three things she wanted, she sat there trying to decide. Finally, with some sadness, she let us know she couldn't decide because she really needed all three to have the set. To her, it was now or never.

My wife and I took the opportunity to point Rikki to God. We showed her how God had given her this opportunity to make money and could give her others. We also helped her to see that any one of the things was wonderful; she didn't need all three.

She understood easily that she needed to trust God to take care of her and be thankful for the things He had already given. We prayed with her and she quickly decided which one to buy. And so we were able to teach the key to contentment to a 6 year old in an immediate and very practical way.

When we as parents continue to take advantage of occasions like these, a foundation is laid that will help our children easily understand the broader application of contentment in all things.

HONESTY IN FINANCES

Two of the first opportunities parents have to teach honesty to a child are rather consistent with all kids. First comes the temptation to tell a lie when the truth will get them in trouble (usually before they understand what a lie is). The second is when, after beginning to realize the value of money, they find some left laying around the house and claim it as their own.

The first occasion is an opportunity to teach children to be honest with what they *say*. The second is an ideal time to begin teaching them to be honest in what they *do*.

As parents we often leap on the first situation: lying is taboo. We tend to be less responsive to the second one. Sometimes we even let the child have the money. To us it's simply pocket change we would have been willing to give them anyway. To them it is much more. The second situation needs as much or more attention than the first.

If we are always honest in what we do, we often will not have reason to be dishonest in what we say. Money innocently picked up off a counter is an ideal opportunity to teach respect for personal property, the value of money, and honesty in dealing with both.

Opportunities to teach God's principles for honesty in a practical way through finances creates stories children never forget. Like that time we drove all the way back to the store because we discovered the clerk hadn't charged us enough. Or the time we waited in line to give the store owner the extra 25 cents the vending machine had given us. If the children remember the story, they remember the lesson.

I (Rick) will never forget the time I learned this lesson. I was minding my Dad's furniture store and sold a lady a wall unit out of one of the supplier's catalogs. I gave her the usual discount off the suggested retail price and she was very happy with it. I wrote up the order and collected a check.

When my Dad returned he checked my numbers and told me he usually gave a bigger discount on that line of furniture. So, when we went to pick up and deliver the unit, Dad wrote a new invoice for $100 less and took a check with him for the customer.

At first I couldn't figure this out. She was happy with the price. It was a good deal. And, (the clincher) we had both agreed on the price. To my mind that made it fair and honest. However, my Dad knew it wasn't consistent with what he usually charged and would charge someone else the next day. Therefore it wasn't honest. That day I learned a lesson in fairness and honesty I've never forgotten and which has translated into every other area of my life.

We can create stories for our children whenever life and the opportunity to do some *financial parenting* give us a pencil and paper.

---

1. "Giving and Volunteering in the United States," Finding from a National Survey 1994 Edition, Washington D.C.

What Spiritually Redeeming Value Does Budgeting Have?

he concepts and principles dealt with in the previous chapter have been pretty straightforward. Now, you might ask, "What can we hope to teach our children while training them in long-term financial planning? or debt and credit management? or even saving and/or investing? beyond, of course, just what's being taught?"

And you may be tempted at this point to add, "You certainly aren't going to tell us there is redeeming value in the principles behind budgeting, are you?"

Actually, these areas represent some of the most important skills required for functioning in life. Unfortunately, they are some of the least taught. They are also one of the primary reasons employers and businesspeople spend so much time and money on seminars billed as teaching the great, secret keys to success. These seminars should be promoted under the byline, "All the Basic Life Skills Everyone Should Really Already Know and Use but They Don't So We're Making a Killing" seminars. It's a little long for a title, probably. Perhaps that's why they just call them, "The Secret Keys to Success."

LONG-TERM FINANCIAL PLANNING

Let's look at this area of long-term planning. Currently, little is being taught about long-term or life planning. It seems to go contrary to everything in our culture that demands immediate attention and instant gratification: life in the now!

When young people are faced with the question of what they want to do with their lives, they find that little they have learned or experienced has prepared them to answer the question. When we begin to teach our children that they need a long-term financial plan, the obvious presents itself: They need a long-term life plan first. When we teach our children to start saving for the long-term, one question leads to the next. Soon they are buzzing with questions that previously hadn't crossed their minds.

God has a plan for each one of us. He created us and gifted us. He knows what we are best suited for. Paul tells us in 1 Corinthians that God places each one of us in a special spot in the body of Christ that is specific to us. It is important for us to teach our children from the time they're old enough to understand that God has a plan for them and wants them, and us, to trust Him with our lives.

This whole concept can be a little vague until we give our children the job of outlining some long-term financial goals. Suddenly it becomes evident. Questions like the following arise: "What does God want me to do?" "Am I going to university or college?" "What about Bible college?" "Am I getting married soon or will it be later?" "How much money will I need to do what God has called me to do?"

The only one who fully knows the answers is God. So the only place questions like these can be resolved is through prayer. Thus, in helping our children understand financial planning, we teach them to pray, consider their options, look at their gifts and potential, and ultimately trust God for wisdom and direction.

The question, "What does God want me to do with my life?" can easily get washed away in our culture's demands to live in the *now*. But while taking our kids through a specific life planning process, using the tools of long-term financial planning, results will be achieved.

The secondary benefit that comes from this process is teaching our children to set goals. A pastor friend once said, "The only difference between a realistic goal and a fantasy is whether or not you have set, and are able to achieve, the intermediate goals or steps that will get you there."

Goal setting gives us the ability to see if we are doing what's necessary in order to achieve the things we believe God has directed us to do. The Bible talks about planning and setting goals.

"The prudent see danger and take refuge, but the simple keep going and suffer for it" (Proverbs 27:12). *"Suppose one of you wants to build a tower. Will he not first sit down and estimate the cost to see if he has enough money to complete it? For if he lays the foundation and is not able to finish it, everyone who sees it will ridicule him, saying, 'This fellow began to build and was not able to finish'"* (Luke 14:28-30).

Jesus knew exactly what He needed to accomplish in His life. He knew all the different stages and events He had to walk through in order to fulfill His Father's will. He did not run His life by just dealing with what came up in the moment. He prepared Himself for His ministry by applying Himself to the learning of God's Word as a youth. He went to John to be baptized and then into the wilderness to be tempted.

Jesus rose in popularity while demonstrating His Father's love and character through His ministry of miracles. He taught people what they needed to know to understand God and His kingdom. He trained those who would begin and establish His church. He opposed the religious leaders and then He walked willingly, knowingly, to the cross. Jesus' cross was what God called Him to. Jesus followed the intermediate steps, achieved all the goals along the way, and arrived at the cross.

The Bible says that in order for us to be Jesus' disciples we have to pick up our crosses and follow Him. Well, we know Jesus died once and for all, so what are the crosses we are to carry? Simply whatever God has called us to achieve for His kingdom in this life. It is *obedience*. If we are to teach our children to follow Jesus' example, we must teach them to seek God and His will. We must help them establish and accomplish intermediate goals for the preparation period, the ministry period, and the final achievement period of what God has called them to do.

It starts with the small opportunities. If we are there to help our children receive a "Well done, good and faithful servant" for what they did today and each day, we don't need to worry about the end of the line. If each day is walked in God's presence and in His will, at the end of life the statement will be "Well done, good and faithful servant!" So, we take it one day at a time!

BORROWING AND LENDING

The biblical use for borrowing and lending was not used as a system for financing. It was an aid to the poor or those who had fallen on hard times. Debt is not recommended in Scripture, although it is not forbidden. It's interesting to note that every mention of borrowing in the Bible is accompanied by a warning. So, in the regular course of God's growth plan for our financial life, ideally, debt should not be in the picture.

The Bible tells us not to be *surety* for others (taking on an obligation to pay without a sure and certain way to pay it—see Proverbs 11:15, 17:18, 20:16).

An example of surety in our day is cosigning loans. There are several reasons we shouldn't cosign loans. One is that the person we're cosigning for may not be able to pay. Although cosigning gives us the false security that we are not really responsible to pay that person's debts, we are! If we have the money it would be better either to lend it to the person ourselves or simply give it to them.

Cosigning gives us the ability to lend (by being responsible for the money) when we cannot afford to, just as borrowing gives us the ability to buy something we really cannot afford.

Another reason is God's system for financial or any other kind of growth. He first helps us to learn and to be proved faithful with a little. Then he gives us more to handle. A financial system that refuses credit to those who can't handle it joins in God's system; it prevents people from getting in over their heads and out of God's progressive growth plan. When we cosign someone's loan, in effect, we have helped that person jump over the hurdles God has placed in front of that person for his or her own safety. We do the same thing to ourselves when we cosign loans that we can't actually afford to pay.

The way credit is used today is the reverse of God's system. "Get the things you need and want now and then grow into the financial responsibility to handle them." There is little motivation to take the hard, safe road to financial security. We've jumped out of God's system in which we trust Him to teach us and give us what we can handle when we can handle it. If easy credit and/or a credit mentality were not prevalent in our society, we would be forced to solve financial problems a different way: the right way.

The right way causes us to look closely at what got us into trouble in the first place. Then, when we find the source of the problem, we can begin dealing with it for good, instead of just for the moment. That's how God's growth plan works for us in the natural course of events. When we violate God's principles, we reap consequences.

It is hoped that we are learning and applying God's principles *before* we get into trouble; but, when the consequences come, we pray for God's wisdom and seek counsel in His Word and from godly people we trust. Then we take what we have learned and begin to apply it and trust God to help us clear up any problem we are now in. That's God's growth process!

The simple core principles behind the proper use of credit can be applied to all the other areas of life. These are important life principles. We can teach them to our children from the springboard of how to properly use credit. When we teach our children to go God's progressive route for growth and when things go wrong examine what they are doing according to His principles (instead of going into debt), we have prepared them for more than just dealing with their finances.

For example, when our children get married there might come a time when their relationships get shaky. The correlation here is interesting. Problems in marriages can be directly paralleled to problems in finances; God's growth plan and principles operate in both.

When we operate according to wrong financial principles, we get into trouble. We seek more money or credit or some other quick fix, we make the problem worse, eventually we run out of options and, if we still don't choose God's principles and fix the problems, we end up in bankruptcy.

In marriages, when our relationships start to go wrong, we seek the same quick fixes. We sometimes ignore the problems by internalizing them or not talking to each other until we've forgotten.

Or, even worse, we begin to close ourselves off from, or harden our hearts toward, our spouses. At this point, another form of relationship debt often takes us deeper into financial debt and we really see the problems mounting. When the marital problems surface, instead of dealing with them we spend money on a night out, a weekend away, or things that make everything seem more pleasant.

There is nothing wrong with spending money or having time away with our spouses. But, if we can't afford it and the real problems are just being whitewashed with a good time, down the road the trouble will simply be amplified. Eventually, just as in finances, if we don't deal with the problems according to God's growth plan, we end up running out of quick-fix options, which may result in marriage bankruptcy, another name for divorce.

On the other hand, the principles learned when we teach our children how to properly use credit will benefit them in *every* area of their lives. The principles give a solid platform to teach from when our children encounter the other areas. While teaching them proper credit and debt management we teach them God's system for dealing with problems. The principles learned in the particular hands-on area of credit management will work in any problem situation in the same way.

Continuing with the marriage example, when our kids apply the principles learned through credit management, instead of just looking for a quick fix, they will be encouraged to seek God, go to His Word, ask for His wisdom and, if necessary, seek godly counsel. Then, instead of their marriages ending in divorce, they will change and operate according to God's principles, and, as a result, they save their marriages.

Another principle we can teach our children while teaching them about credit and debt is faithfulness. We can teach them to only make commitments they can keep and always to be faithful to keep commitments made. There is a saying in Africa, "A promise is a debt." It's very true. A commitment is a serious thing.

Establishing these truths might sound like huge and ominous life principles to teach our kids, but when we bring it down to the specific area of teaching them not to allow debt, and why, it becomes easy to lay the foundation.

SAVING AND INVESTING

What foundational principles can we teach our children through training in the area of saving and investing? First, we can teach that it is not unspiritual to save. Nor does it mean a lack of faith. This is one principle that we, as God's people, need to learn and practice more. By putting money into savings we can store money to use for future needs. All too often we use credit instead.

Credit is the reverse of savings. Using credit means buying a product now and trying to pay the purchase price later. Unfortunately, interest charges are added to the purchase price, which makes payment even more difficult.

A far better concept taught in God's Word is sacrifice in the short term for long-term goals. It's important to plan for and budget some savings. Otherwise, using credit becomes a lifelong necessity and debt becomes a way of life. Savings allows us to buy with cash and shop for the best deals.

When we teach our children to save to buy something instead of getting it on credit, we teach them two basic financial principles: responsibility and wisdom in stewardship and a clearer understanding of money as a means of exchange. These two principles help lay the foundation for another incredible life-changing and foundational principle. But let's deal with the first two points first.

When we buy something using credit, often we are buying on impulse or we've made an I-have-to-have-it or I-deserve-it decision. These conditions are the least compatible with wise buying. Our emotions, rather than our wisdom, are driving the purchase. With this motivation it's hard to stop and examine the decision. Nor are we likely to wait for a sale or to compare prices.

One of the main reasons all of this takes place is because we've lost track of the value of our money. This happens because when we just sign our names on credit slips it doesn't seem like we're spending our money. And, right at that moment, we're not. The realization of the lack of wisdom involved in our purchases hits when the thrill of the item has waned, when the item is worn out or broken, but the payments still have to be made.

Now look at the other side. When we work hard and sacrifice in order to save for the things we want, we have time to make an informed, time-tempered decision. Another interesting thing happens: When we've saved the money over a period of time, we have a real understanding of the value of each dollar. Our attitudes change and our desire to get the best value increases substantially.

Try testing this on your kids. One week tell them they can spend a certain amount of their savings during a shopping trip. Another day give them the same amount of money and tell them they can use it any way they want. You can guess what the results will be.

One of the things we are helping and preparing our children to learn, when we teach them to save, is stewardship responsibility. We've cleared away the fog of credit and instant decision making. We are helping them see money as a means of exchange and how important it is for them to be responsible stewards with each decision. (Remember, ultimately, it's God's money.)

One of the best things we can do in teaching this process to young children is to make all purchasing decisions before going shopping. We can tell the children, "We are going to buy groceries for next week. If you would like to buy yourself a treat (name a purchase price limit) you may, but we won't be making any other purchases today." Once we've done this a few times the rule will be well established and the children will understand they cannot get everything they want with the money allowed. This gives us an opportunity to discuss their shopping decisions with them. If they want something that costs more than they are allowed to spend on this trip, we can help them plan and save for when they will have enough to buy what they want.

When we teach our children how to plan ahead for the future and save enough to fulfill their plans, they will be less prone to emotional, impulse buying that can take their plans off track. They also will see the results and feel good about themselves and the decisions they have made.

Now here's that incredible life-changing foundational principle our children have already begun to learn: Make every decision a good decision by considering God's principles, because every decision affects the future.

We need to help younger children reach their goals and feel fulfilled. However, we must not rescue older children from bad purchasing decisions. They need to experience the consequences of their actions.

My (Larry's) second son learned this lesson as a young teen. We had given our two oldest sons their clothing money and, after instructing them in wise buying, dropped them off at the mall with some anxiety. Two hours later we met them as arranged. The oldest son had bought sensibly. The second one had bought some socks. He thought his clothes were fine for the next six months and had used the rest of the money for a skateboard. We decided to let him experience the consequences of his decision, so we didn't return the skateboard.

Learning to use a skateboard involves a fair amount of falling, foot scraping, and general wear-and-tear on the clothes. Just as school was about to resume in September, the skateboarding son took stock of his clothes. His jeans had holes in the knees, and his toes were protruding from his sneakers. He went to school like that. This was embarrassing both for him and for us, as his parents. However, during the months leading up to the next clothing allotment, he learned that his spending decisions have consequences.

By letting our children experience the results of their own decisions (in a safe context), we are teaching them to consider future consequences. When tempted to spend foolishly later, they will have learned it's better to plan and wait. In this way they will learn to make decisions based on God's principles and long-term effects, as opposed to making them in the heat of the moment.

At this point, with this solid foundation established, our children are ready to face other, far more damaging temptations and peer pressures. And we have built the platform that will enable us to help them make tougher choices with their future in mind instead of letting instant gratification or emotional satisfaction act as their guides.

The art of disciplining a child is to successfully lead them through simple decisions, instruct them in God's principles, and help them quickly receive and recognize rewards and/or consequences as teaching aids. When we punish our children, we don't want to leave them with the understanding that they were punished because they didn't do what we said and we're bigger than they are.

When we punish a child, we are showing him or her instantly what the Bible teaches: When we follow God's principles good things happen and rewards are forthcoming, but when we violate His principles things don't work out for us because things go wrong and penalties are unavoidable. Now our children can believe us when we say, "I hate this as much as you do. But I have to punish you now to keep you from greater trouble and punishments later in your life. I do this because I love you. I want the best for you."

"He who spares the rod hates his son, but he who loves him is careful to discipline him" (Proverbs 13:24). In this case, we as parents can use the discipline of saving money and spending it wisely to show our love and teach our children greater principles that will keep them from a world of hurt.

As our children get older, investing money can be used to communicate these same principles. We will make sure they have a long-term goal or plan for their investments and help them invest wisely. More importantly, we will help them stick with their investment plan when they would like to change their minds and spend the money on something now.

THE "B" WORD (BUDGETING)

We started this chapter wondering what godly and wonderful principle possibly could flourish out of the sometimes laborious task of budgeting. We were being facetious because budgeting *can* help us establish a fortress of God's principles in our children's lives. The first thing we do is teach simple foundational things for children to get hold of and then, once that has been learned, we move them on.

In order for anything else we've talked about so far to make any sense to our children we must teach them to separate their money into *purpose categories* as soon as they get it. That's called budgeting.

It's the foundation of foundations for every other financial parenting principle we've taught. Even for the youngest children, money must be separated into these purpose categories so they know what they should give, what they should save, and what they should spend. Once they have done this, our kids must learn to fulfil their commitments to the categories. This is the foundation both for *self-control*, keeping ones' commitments to God and oneself, and *faithfulness*, keeping ones' commitments to God and others.

We've talked about how long-term financial planning becomes the platform for teaching our children to seek God's plan for their lives. We discussed how learning intermediate goal setting is the undergirding of that foundation. Well, what about budgeting? What can it teach? It's simple. Without an immediate plan for this week and this month, we cannot gauge if our intermediate goals and long-term plans are on track or even attainable.

Perhaps the most important thing budgeting can establish in our children's lives is the obvious parallel. That is, how the decisions and actions they make today and this month are going to affect where they will be going and what God has for them.

Time management and life management parallel budgeting exactly. Children or young people who can learn to *make a plan and work their plan*, who can plan their lives and their time and then live their plans with their time, are people who will achieve under God's hand. If we can simply start on the basics of budgeting and then transfer those principles to time and life management, we will see great results.

Budgeting for kids starts out as dividing their money into simple purpose categories. Likewise, we can help children see that their lives have different purpose categories. This is a foundation for teaching them a daily devotional habit, helping them make decisions about when to get homework and chores done, and how they can then have free time. How many of us have taught our children that they must plan and then spend time developing relationships with God, with family, and with friends? Budgeting is a great place, a necessary place, to begin teaching our kids a wealth of wisdom!

Another great benefit to teaching our children all of these different financial foundational principles is the sense of confidence and security it will give them. When our children realize that life is run by fundamental principles they already have learned in these simple areas, practical life becomes less intimidating. This will give them a sense of direction, confidence, and value in Christ that will help them succeed in whatever God has called and gifted them to do.

The reason money and wealth are not to be our goal isn't because these things are evil. Rather, it's because, by allowing ourselves or our children to focus our energies there, we might compromise God's principles and, therefore, our stewardship to get them. But if pleasing God—which is stewardship—is our goal and our children's, we will learn through the application of God's principles in finances. Then we will go on to apply those principles in every area of our lives and find out what true wealth and riches really are.

In 1993, 28.5 million adolescents in the United States spent $28 billion and influenced another $155 billion in family spending. (Some estimates go as high as spending $90 billion and influencing another $200 billion!)

The new hang-out for teens is the shopping malls. A nationwide survey showed that, when looking for shopping, socializing with friends, or simply for entertainment, nine out of ten teens head for the local mall. While at the mall, teens spend an average of $32.68 per visit. Look at how it is broken down:

young teens - less than $10.00 per visit
middle teens - $16 to $40 per visit

older teens - $41 to $50 per visit.

The average teen makes three trips to the mall each month.

Few children or teens do anything with their money besides spend it. Nor are they taught to do differently. One survey shows that more than 66 percent of kids run out of money at least once a month and 50 percent run out every week. These figures show the principles we as a nation are teaching, intentionally or unintentionally, to our kids.

- Live for today.
- Your life is defined by what and how much you have.
- The purpose of life is pleasure and consumption.
- There is no need to plan for tomorrow; the government will take care of everything.
- The mall has become our kids' church and sales flyers and catalogs their Bible.

The concept of *financial parenting* is so simple. Let's summarize.

It is based on God's growth principles: We teach our kids to apply His principles in simple areas with simple responsibilities and relatively simple rewards and consequences, and from there we go on to help them apply the same principles to more difficult areas. Our children see results from applying God's principles in an easy-to-understand, hands-on application and can be made to see that they can apply the same principles and expect the same kind of results in more difficult areas and situations. Finances is an excellent "first discipline" because it is distinct and hands-on.

"For where your treasure is, there your heart will be also" (Matthew 6:21). We need to teach our children where to bury their treasures. Then we need to encourage them and watch their hearts follow. The result will be children who are not only wise stewards but strong believers too.

The Approach

How Can We Get All This Across to Our Children?

*Y*ou have probably heard the saying, "It's the thought that counts!" But have you ever seen an actual situation where that was true? James says that faith without works is dead. The kind thought or intention without the deed is dead.

Also, the thought and the deed can be ruined when the presentation betrays or miscommunicates the motivation. For example, let's say you buy your wife flowers or your husband his favorite magazine and chocolate bar because you want to make up for something you did. You walk in, turn on the television, and throw the gift in front of your spouse as you mutter, "Okay. So I was a jerk. Let's get on with life." No matter how good your thoughts and intentions were, you blew the presentation. And don't try to rescue it at this point by saying, "Hey, it's the thought that counts!"

Financial parenting or parenting of any kind is the same: It's not just the thought that counts; the effort and the presentation of the effort are what get the job done.

"If I speak in the tongues of men and of angels, but have not love, I am only a resounding gong or a clanging cymbal. If I have the gift of prophecy and can fathom all mysteries and all knowledge, and if I have a faith that can move mountains, but have not love, I am nothing. If I give all I possess to the poor and surrender my body to the flames, but have not love, I gain nothing" (1 Corinthians 13:1-3).

If we could be perfect parents, as far as our performance goes, and teach our children to accomplish all the great things listed in these verses, without love it will not have gained us anything or made us or our children into anything. Paul isn't knocking these accomplishments, or accomplishments in general; nor is he advocating love without action. There are two conclusive statements in these verses that we need to examine more closely: *"but have not love, I am nothing"* and *"but have not love, I gain nothing."*

Jesus said the two greatest, most important commandments are to love God and to love others. These two, He said, sum up everything else God has ever commanded us to do. Since God is love and completely unselfish, everything He tells us to do is for our good, not His. Therefore, the two greatest commands help us see where our focus should be and where the true blessings of life are.

The greatest thing a person can do in this life is to develop a love relationship with God. The second is to develop relationships with others and love them: families, friends, brothers and sisters in Christ. These two things are what bring fulfillment. A loving relationship with God and loving relationships with others is what life is really all about; the rest is all sets and props.

Paul's two defining statements provide us with a focus: First, *"but have not love, I am nothing."* You've heard it said, "It's not what you know but who you know that counts." In one sense that's what Paul is saying. Who we are is not defined by what we know, the things we understand, our knowledge of future events, or the amount of faith we have. It's defined by the loving relationships we have and the love between ourselves and God.

To see more clearly what Paul was saying, consider the life and death of a certain businessman. The man was very successful in business and had accumulated quite a bit of wealth. However, the rest of his life was less than perfect. The pastor of a nearby church was asked to conduct the funeral service. He attempted to find out something about this man from his family. His children refused to talk to the pastor or to attend his funeral. His wife did not want to talk about him either. She went to the funeral, only because it was a legal requirement that someone be present. In fact, she refused to accommodate her husband's one request for his funeral: to have the song, "I Did It My Way" sung. This man's accomplishments are listed for posterity. But how do we assess his life? Whether fair or unfair, we probably assess who this man was by the attendance and atmosphere at the funeral. This man was, in that sense, *"nothing."*

Paul's second statement is *"but have not love, I gain nothing."* This statement comes after an impressive list of things done or accomplished. Yet these gain nothing. So the real things in this life to be gained and focused on are loving relationships with God and loving relationships with others here and now. Anything else or any other goal is missing the point. We can see, then, that it's not the thought or even just the effort that counts.

Love exists to develop relationships. Its purpose is not only to define the tone of voice we use to speak to others or to govern how we react to others; a person can learn to be polite and cordial and still be full of hate. So, if we do something for another but it hasn't communicated our love and blessed them so that our relationship is advanced, we are a *resounding gong* and a *clanging cymbal.*

Paul used a similar metaphor one chapter later when he was talking about praying in public. He said, *"If the trumpet does not sound a clear call, who will get ready for battle?"* (1 Corinthians 14:8). If the demonstration of our love, our efforts, our lives, and our pursuits do not further relationships, we are and have gained nothing.

The two commandments don't say and don't mean "think loving thoughts and feel nice feelings for God and others"; the two commandments send us on a quest for love relationships. *"Love the Lord your God with all your heart, soul, mind and strength."* That's commitment to relationship. And the other, *"Love others as yourself."* Paul said in Ephesians 5:29 that we don't hate our own bodies; we feed and care for them.

Love, then, goes beyond feelings and one-way gestures. The two greatest commands call us to the two greatest responsibilities and the two greatest blessings in life: relationship with God and relationship with others!

The last verse in 1 Corinthians chapter 13 says, *"And now these three remain: faith, hope and love. But the greatest of these is love."* Faith gives us the ability to believe and live according to what God says is true. Hope shows us where we are going. Love defines our purpose for being, our goals for this life and the next, our priorities, and our ultimate reward. Love is the greatest.

When it comes to *financial parenting*, this affects us in everything we do. The way we approach our kids must be with and in love. Everything we do must enhance our relationship with our children, thereby strengthening trust and the desire they have to learn from us and follow our examples. Without this we will accomplish nothing.

Financial parenting is, simply, teaching our children God's principles in every part of their lives, starting with the most basic and practical, then helping them apply those principles to every other area as they grow.

This chapter is about approach: the best way to teach our children. All of the principles of approach covered are grounded in love—the concept of developing a love relationship with our kids. This is the *foundation.*

Financial parenting requires hands-on teaching and training skills. These are, in actuality, key parenting skills. Somewhere along the path of progressive generational thought we got the idea it was the government's, school board's, society's, and church's responsibility to teach our kids. Not so. It is our job as parents. We have others to help us but we are the primary trainers and teachers. We are ultimately responsible to see the job gets done.

So we need to apply ourselves to becoming better teachers (which is becoming better parents) and to applying parenting principles. The principle of love defines and engulfs all other principles.

A LOVE STITCH IN THEIR HEARTS AT NINE WILL SAVE THE ADULT COUNSELORS A LOT OF TIME

A child is a "trust." We are stewards of our children's lives for a short time. When God requires them to obey and follow us as parents, He requires that we follow Him.

We need to treat our children as if they are God's children and we are just temporary baby-sitters. We use the word baby-sitter to conjure up a familiar picture. Recall the moment when the parents arrive home and the baby-sitter is asked, "How did it go?" That baby-sitter knows this is the moment of accountability. A positive report about the kids is great. But the nervousness comes from the real underlying question, "How did you do?" "Did you treat my children well?"

If the thought of God coming to pick up His "kids" today and asking us and them how it went is a little unnerving, we can pray and ask for His forgiveness and help. God wants the best for us and our children—that's *grace parenting*. He's ready to help.

We need to treat and teach our children with respect as fellow heirs to God's kingdom and as budding young children of God. Sometimes we forget that how we treat our children, what we say and do, will be remembered by them when they are adults, just as we remember events in our earlier years.

We need to reflect a loving, forgiving, Father God in our parenting. As He is patient and kind with us, so we need to be patient and kind with our children. As He forgives and instructs, so we are to forgive and gently instruct.

James 1:5 says, *"If any of you lacks wisdom, he should ask God, who gives generously to all without finding fault, and it will be given to him."* Without finding fault. That means when we go to God for wisdom He doesn't say, "It's about time you came around! Do you know how stupid you've been?" No. He says, "I love you," and He begins to instruct us from that point forward, lovingly teaching and guiding us.

We need to demonstrate our love for and our patience with our children as we lovingly instruct them. At the same time, we must not go so far with what we think is love that we stop training and disciplining our children. If we don't discipline and correct them, the Bible says we don't love them. *"He who spares the rod hates his son, but he who loves him is careful to discipline him"* (Proverbs 13:24).

A love stitch in their hearts at nine will save the adult counselors a lot of time. A solid base of consistent love and discipline establishes solid and balanced parent-child relationships.

We explain God's principles to our children by using the ingredients for foundational teaching:

- What the Bible says,
- Simple words and real life examples and allegories,
- The reason and Ruler behind the rule.

For example, if we are teaching our children about tithing, we may want to tell them the story of Abraham giving a tithe to Melchizedek in Genesis 14. It's a story, so it will hold their interest and be easier for them to remember. (We may want to read it ourselves and retell it, depending on our children's ages.) We can explain how Abraham was showing everyone that it was God who helped him win this battle by giving a tenth of everything back to God.

Now we draw the parallel to ourselves by reading *"Honor the Lord with your wealth, with the firstfruits of all your crops; then your barns will be filled to overflowing, and your vats will brim over with new wine"* (Proverbs 3:9-10). We can tell our children that, like Abraham, when we tithe we show we believe God owns everything and He is the one who takes care of us. Then we tell them a real life story of how we began to tithe and some ways God took care of us. Also, if they are too young to understand percentages, we can get out a dollar and ten dimes and physically demonstrate what we mean.

Next, take the time to explain the reason and Ruler behind the rule. Explain simply that this money helps the church pay its bills and its pastors and help needy people. We should explain this is important to God because He loves us and the people our money is helping. He invented church to help us become stronger Christians. We also can explain that God loves us and wants to take care of us. When we obey Him we show Him we want Him to do just that.

Now that we've explained the concept to our children, we need to show it to them. We can let them see us prepare our tithes. If we can show it visibly, we should let them see that the tithe is the first line in our budget; it's the first thing we do when we get our money. We can let them help us put the money in the envelope and, if possible, put the envelope in the offering at church. We can point out the pastors our money will help. We might explain how it will help them buy food and clothes.

After teaching the principle of tithing, we need to help our children implement tithing practically in their own lives. We don't just tell them to do it, we walk through it with them. We show them how to separate their own money to give God His part and remind them to put it in the offering at church.

Now that we've started our kids tithing, we need to consistently help them with it. We need to reinforce the principles and the teaching behind the principles at regular intervals. For example, we can pray together on the way to church. We can thank God for taking care of us and our family and for the opportunity to give to the people at church. When our children are ready and curious, we can teach them more on the topic from the Bible. We need to look and pray for the opportunities.

Also, a really important part of parenting is to watch for and identify God at work. For example, if God opens up an opportunity for our children to earn more money, or they get an incredible deal on something they have been saving for, or some money comes to them through an unexpected channel, we can point it out to our children as a way God has honored their faith and obedience and has taken care of them.

We have shown that how we approach our children when teaching them about God and His ways is crucial. Whatever the topic we want to impart—from potty training to financial management—we need to approach our children in ways that will make it easy for them to learn and will make the process as enjoyable as possible.

As we conclude this chapter, let me suggest that you reflect on the following facts.

CHAPTER SEVEN

- Our motivation is love.
- Our guidebook is God's Word.
- Our lives are the example.
- Our attitudes are that of fellow learners.
- Our platform for teaching is life.
- Our methods are unique to our students.
- Our message is clear and plain.

Practical Tips, Suggestions, Tools, and Activities

Lay the Foundations

*N*ow we get down to the practical helps: tips, ideas, and resources for getting the job done.

Many books have been written on the subject of teaching our kids about the practical way to save, open a bank account, invest, write checks, balance a bank statement, and so on. We will cover some of that. However, our goal in this section is to give the tips and suggestions needed for passing on to our kids what the Bible teaches about finances.

For each financial topic we will arm you with related Bible stories, memory verses, and practical ideas and activities that not only teach finances but also point our children to God and His principles. We want to help you take them beyond financial applications to the broader life application of the principles learned. When we establish the truth of the entire Bible, and then the individual truths of the Bible, we prepare our children to fight error with truth.

Children should learn first the difference between *needs, wants,* and *desires. Needs* are the purchases necessary to provide basic requirements, such as food, clothing, a job, home, medical coverage, and others. *"But if we have food and clothing, we will be content with that"* (1 Timothy 6:8).

Wants involve choices about the quality of goods to be used: dress clothes versus work clothes, steak versus hamburger, a new car versus a used car. There's a point of reference for determining wants in a Christian's life: *"Your beauty should not come from outward adornment, such as braided hair and the wearing of gold jewelry and fine clothes. Instead, it should be that of your inner self, the unfading beauty of a gentle and quiet spirit, which is of great worth in God's sight"* (1 Peter 3:3-4).

Desires are choices according to God's plan that can be made only out of *surplus* funds—after all other obligations have been met. *"Do not love the world or anything in the world. If anyone loves the world, the love of the Father is not in him. For everything in the world—the cravings of sinful man, the lust of his eyes and the boasting of what he has and does—comes not from the Father but from the world. The world and its desires pass away, but the man who does the will of God lives forever"* (1 John 2:15-17).

Now, before we roll up our sleeves and get into the details, we'd like to help you develop a *parenting economic plan* that will establish a framework and ground rules from which you can teach.

Before we can teach children what to do with their money, they need to have some. To give them an allowance or not: that is the next question.

PARENTING ECONOMICS 101

Parenting Economics Rule #1. **The family is a community: everyone in the family shares in the opportunities, responsibilities, rewards, and income of that community.**

Some experts feel that giving a child an allowance, but not tying it to effort, helps establish in them a something-for-nothing attitude. Other experts argue that tying a regular payment to household chores destroys the idea of community effort and establishes an I-need-to-be-paid-for-everything-I-do attitude. The key is to give our children an allowance and require them to do their household duties without tying the two together like a work-for-hire agreement. As part of a family or a community, we take on certain responsibilities and gain certain benefits.

We need to teach our children that everyone in a family contributes responsibly to the overall running of the household or community. For example, when our children come out with "but I didn't make that mess" or something similar, we can use the opportunity to give them a reality check.

We can point out the multitude of household jobs—doing dishes, cleaning floors, cleaning bathrooms, doing the laundry, gardening, dusting, painting—that provide everyone's needs, not just one person's. Our children should be responsible for more than cleaning up after themselves.

The Bible says, *"Each of you should look not only to your own interests, but also to the interests of others"* (Philippians 2:4). The family community benefits are food, shelter, clothing, relationship, and also an allowance. Since the children's allowance should not be tied to specific tasks as payment, it can be explained as follows.

- The income that is earned for the family is household and community income and is to be used for that purpose.

- As part of the family or community, children receive an

income (or allowance) until they have income of their own. One of the primary purposes for this income is to help them begin to learn how to handle finances.

One of the big advantages to be gained by starting out this way is that we won't be in trouble later from difficult inconsistencies when our children's community responsibilities increase and their allowance eventually becomes nonexistent.

So, the next question is, if our children are not keeping up their end of the responsibilities, should their community income cease? Yes, but only in the context of teaching community responsibility. It should be a last resort.

We need to train our kids, encourage them, and help them grow in their responsibilities. This is much better than just telling them to do something and then yanking privileges when they don't do it right. We should consider whether we have ever taught them how to do the job. Have we shown them how to do it? Have we helped them establish a system and a schedule for doing it? Have we taught them how to enjoy their work and take pride in a job well done? If the answer to any of these questions concerning the job our children are falling down on is "No," perhaps we should consider suspending our own allowances.

Remember, it's our job as parents not only to instruct but to train. I couldn't expect to tell my daughter how to play the piano, put her in front of an audience, and then punish her for not being able to give a piano concert. And, just telling my son how to play football would not win him an MVP award.

Learning how to work hard, do a job well, and do specific jobs well takes time, patience, and personal-support training. By teaching that the family is a community of people working and living together for mutual growth and benefit, and putting allowances in that light, we establish right attitudes and principles.

So, allowances can be given with two understandings: An

allowance is a benefit of living in the family community, and each person living in this community has responsibilities around the house, such as specific jobs: keeping his or her room clean, washing dishes, taking out the garbage, folding the laundry, dusting the furniture, and so on.

***Parenting Economics Rule #2*. Establish job opportunities inside and outside the home that serve as a training ground for individual work and remuneration.**

How then can we begin to teach our children a work ethic and the idea that work equals pay? We do this by giving our kids the opportunity to earn extra money doing jobs that go beyond cleaning up after themselves or fulfilling their share of family or community responsibilities. We will cover this in more detail later in this section under "Diligence."

***Parenting Economics Rule #3*. Be sure allowances do not discourage joy in community involvement nor encourage laziness.**

In order to ensure a balance between family community involvement and individual work for remuneration, we need to be careful about setting allowance amounts. Children's allowances should be enough to look forward to, enough to enable us to begin teaching budgeting, but not enough that all their wants and desires are met so they have no need for extra jobs. For this reason allowances may have to be reviewed and adjusted from time to time.

Ultimately, we need to wean our children off allowances and onto their own earned income. Therefore we need to be sure our raises don't keep pace, percentage-wise, with their budgets. Their allowances should become an ever-decreasing portion of their budget.

Parenting Economics Rule #4. **Be consistent in the teaching, training, and disciplining process.**

Consistency and diligence is our part of the process. Once we have established an allowance amount and frequency, we need to add it into our family budget and pay it as we would any other bill—consistently and on time. Also, if we establish a rule for our kids, with rewards and penalties for the compliance and/or non-compliance of that rule, it is essential that we always, always follow through.

Parenting Economics Rule #5. **Let everything we do reflect real life as closely as possible—its systems, its rewards, and its penalties.**

For example, we shouldn't pay our children for a job that is half done or not done well. Rather, if they still need training, we can help them complete the job but not pay until it is finished. In the job market we don't get half pay for half a job. We get no pay and/or we lose our jobs.

Parenting Economics Rule #6. **Take the cloaking devices off family finances.**

It's important to let our kids know about, see the workings of, and get involved in family and household finances.

Parenting Economics Rule #7. **When assigning tasks, giving job opportunities, and deciding on training and discipline methods, take the individual child into consideration—strengths, weaknesses, abilities, and problems.**

Sometimes, when we think we've run up against bad attitudes in our children, we may be dealing with misunderstood aptitudes. Some very good books have been written on understanding our children's personality types, learning methods, aptitudes, giftings, and even how their birth order affects who they are. One thing is for sure. Kids are not born as blanks for us to program. God made each one unique.

We don't need psychology degrees to understand the basics of this principle. In making people, God used some basic personality patterns and learning styles. We as parents can do a better job by having a simple understanding of them. For example, some personality types are very meticulous and detailed; they love to count and budget every penny. This type may find the idea of budgeting easy but may need encouragement to actually spend some of their neatly counted money. Another personality type may need more visual activities, discipline, simpler budget categories, and a lot of encouragement to budget.

Another thing to consider is gender. God made males and females different. Our daughters' motivational triggers will be different from our sons', just as the things they'll want to spend their money on will be different. It's important to be careful not to compare our children's strengths and weaknesses to their siblings'. We must deal with each child as an individual and ask God for individual wisdom.

Let's draw the balance here. Our personality differences and uniqueness are never valid excuses for violating God's laws or principles. We are all responsible to follow God's principles, so we must never make excuses for our kids in this area. The method of training the various personality types and the application of principles can be tailored. Some good books on these topics can be found in the resource list in the Appendix.

Now, let's get practical. In this section we will discuss how we can teach and train our children in twelve financial areas. We have grouped the twelve areas into four categories. The first category includes *stewardship, trusting God, tithing/giving,* and *generosity.* These are the bedrock foundations for managing our finances according to God's Word.

The second group includes *contentment, honesty,* and *diligence.* These are areas in which the foundations are worked inward into our hearts and attitudes. The third and fourth groups are the more outward, external working out of the foundations.

The third group has to do with organization and planning: *long-term financial planning* and *budgeting.*

The fourth group includes *saving/investing, spending,* and *credit/debt.*

For each area we will provide some tools for the practical teaching and training that needs to be done. These are intended as starting points and do not attempt to lay out everything that needs to be or can be done to teach an area. They will provide a framework within which to train and some ideas to get you going. We will use the following tools.

Family Motto

When I (Rick) was teaching my kids about telling the truth and keeping their word, we developed a family motto. "If I say it, I'll do it. If I say it, it's the truth. You can count on it!" It was not only quickly memorized by everyone, but it seemed to have a profound effect in that the kids could identify with this being a special saying for our family. Of course, we grounded it in God's Word, but its uniqueness to our family was key. It helped, especially as a guide reference point, when a reminder was needed. You can use the motto we suggest or make up one of your own.

Bible Story

When teaching a lesson or principle from God's Word, a story from the Bible to illustrate the lesson strengthens the concept and makes it more solid. We have endeavored to give a Bible story, its reference, and a wrap-up that will help draw out the lesson. There are, of course, many other Bible stories that could be used to reinforce the teaching.

Faith Story

We also advise that the Bible story be followed with a personal faith story that illustrates the lesson. Although we give suggestions, you'll have to supply the actual story.

Memory Verse

The reason children memorize Bible verses shouldn't be so they can get extra stickers or bonus points at Sunday School. Memorizing the Bible is for a deeper purpose: so we can readily refer to it when we have life decisions to make. We need to help our children to not only memorize but understand these Scriptures so God's Spirit can use the verses to guide them when they have financial decisions to make. Remember, since the purpose of a memory verse is its application, understanding it is more important than word-for-word accuracy.

Definition

We give a simple definition of the word and principle. These are written in language children will understand. You can use them as an aid or simply read them to your children. Then, if needed, you can explain the concept further.

Tips

These give practical advice on how to incorporate the principles into your family life and the training process.

Activities

These are ideas for hands-on things you can do with your kids to assist in the teaching and training process. They should be fun as well as educational. Again, these are suggestions to get you started. Some may not work for your family, but perhaps they will give you other ideas.

Pointers

Suggestions and reminders for how to point your children toward applying the principle in other areas of their lives.

STEWARDSHIP

Family Motto

"We're looking after (our money), for the Master."

Bible Story

The faithful stewards (Luke 19:12-26)

We can read this parable with our children and explain that God gives us things to care for. He wants us to use them wisely, according to His principles. If God owns what we have, then we must use it the way He wants us to. God does it this way because He loves us and knows how things will work out the best. When we are obedient with what He gives us, He will be able to trust us with more.

Faith Story

Tell the kids a story about a time you chose to follow God's instructions instead of your own ideas and how everything worked out.

Memory Verse

"The earth is the Lord's, and everything in it, the world, and all who live in it" (Psalm 24:1).

Definition

Stewardship means that God owns everything. He gives us

things to look after (to manage). Since everything belongs to God, we need to take care of what we have the way He tells us to in the Bible. When we do that, we can trust God to take care of us and God can trust us with more. We should want to be the best stewards we can possibly be for God.

Tips

1. When making a purchasing decision, we can pray a simple prayer out loud for our kids to hear. First we can tell God we want to be good stewards. Then we can ask Him for wisdom and direction in our purchasing decision.

2. When our families are faced with major decisions, such as moving, buying a home, replacing a car, changing careers, or even deciding what to do with surplus income, we can pray together as families and let the children in on how God directs.

Activities

Play the "It All Belongs to God" game. (Parents should play the game too.)

Take out scissors, paper, pencils, and glue, as well as old magazines and newspapers. Find one big piece of paper or cardboard and put it in the center of the table. Have everyone draw or find pictures or words that represent everything the family owns, from the house to the kids' toys. Next, glue or tape them down in a collage all over the paper or cardboard.

If your kids are too old for this, have everyone write a list and see who can come up with the longest list in a certain time period. Doing it room by room in the house and awarding points for each room could add fun. See who the winner is when you've finished going through the house.

It's important to explain from the start the purpose for doing this: so that we can give it back to God. When you're finished with the collage or lists, you can pray a short prayer together, thanking God for everything He's made you stewards over (managers of). Then you can give it all back to Him again and ask for His wisdom and guidance in using it.

Now, clean up the clutter and have a treat of some kind or do something the kids really like to do. It's important not to belabor a teaching activity. When you've finished, emphasize the point of the activity; then give a reward of some kind.

Pointers

When playing the "It All Belongs to God" game, add words or representational pictures for intangible things, such as life, family, relationships, friends, salvation, talents, careers, and so on, to the collage.

In the older-age version of the game, we can do an intangible room and have everyone make their lists. Our goal is to help the young people take the concept of God giving us things to care for, beyond the physical, to include everything we have—even ourselves and our lives. When they understand how all of who we are and what we have belongs to God, we can help our children pray for direction and wisdom in all these areas.

TRUSTING GOD

Family Motto

"In God we trust! He always looks after us."

Bible Story

God takes care of us (read what Jesus said about God taking care of us in Matthew 6:25-34). Follow it up with the coin in the fish's mouth story (Matthew 17:24-27).

We can explain to our children that Jesus always knew His

Father would look after Him. Jesus wants us to trust God to take care of us as well. God wants us to obey Him and follow His principles. Since God knows how everything works best, things will work out better when we follow the "instruction manual" (Bible).

It's not our obedience or following His principles that ensures we are taken care of. God cares for us because He loves us, pure and simple. When it doesn't look like God's ways of doing things are working, that's when we really need to trust Him, know He loves us, and trust He is working things out.

Faith Story
Tell your kids about a time God met a financial need of yours.

Memory Verse
"And my God will meet all your needs according to his glorious riches in Christ Jesus" (Philippians 4:19).

Definition
When we *trust* someone, it means we know they will do what is right, or they will do what they said they would do.

Suppose someone tells us he or she will buy us lunch. If we know this person always does what he or she says, then we won't make a lunch for ourselves that day. We trust the person to keep his or her word and buy us lunch.

If our moms ask us to taste something, we don't have to wonder if it is something yucky, like mashed worms. We trust our moms because we know they love us.

Jesus told us that God loves us and we can trust Him to take care of us. There are three important things to remember about trusting God. First, if we really trust Him, we'll do things the way He tells us they should be done (just like we trust our moms when they ask us to taste). Second, because God knows everything, and we know just a very little, sometimes the things God does don't make sense or aren't the way we want things to work out. We need to keep trusting Him anyway because, third, He really does love us and it will work out if we keep trusting Him. We can pray about everything, ask God to please work things out, and ask Him for wisdom. There may be something He needs us to do.

When it comes to money, we need to do the same thing: follow God's ways for handling our money. Then we can trust He will take care of us and work things out. We pray and ask Him about the things we need or the things we don't understand. We ask Him for wisdom and keep trusting Him, no matter what.

Remember, we also need to trust God when it comes to how much money He's given us. He may give us wisdom to be wiser with what we have instead of answering our prayers for more.

Tips

1. We should always encourage our children to take every one of their concerns to God and talk to Him about them. We can encourage them to ask Him for wisdom and direction.

2. We should help our kids look into what the Bible says about what they should do or about what God will do for them in and through their situations.

3. Once they know they are doing things God's way, we can consistently point our kids toward trusting God. We want to help them avoid worry—by praying together with them and reminding them of God's faithfulness. Now's a good time to tell them about a time when you trusted God, even though it was hard, and how everything eventually worked out.

4. When we go through a time when things don't look good and we determine to trust God through it, we can share the process with our kids and rejoice with them when God works it out.

Activities

Ask God to help you come up with a "trust project" for the whole family. Noah and his family were involved in a trust project! A family trust project can, of course, be less intense than building an ark, but the results can still be great.

• Although a trust project could be something like redecorating the Sunday school room, most will involve things you are called to do (although Noah built the ark, your task might be supporting a missionary) or things your family is going through (the need for a reliable vehicle, money for a fence, or replacing the television set). Financial trouble in the family is a great trust project and involving your kids will help you to keep on trusting, even through the tough times.

• Often, one of your giving projects will require trusting God for provision, wisdom, and working out details. Combined giving and trust projects are great. Trust projects can be anything you are trusting God with. The key is to involve your kids in the process.

Pointers

Once we have taught our kids about trust, demonstrated it in our lives, and have involved them in a trust project, they will have an easier time with personal trust projects. This is when we encourage them to trust God to meet their needs and answer their prayers.

Once we have established the trust project process, we can encourage them to apply it to every area of life. Helping them to apply it to a friendship that looks like it's falling apart will prepare them, later, to look at marriage as a trust project.

Also, once our kids truly understand God's love and trustworthiness the next principles will come easier. It's easier to give, for example, when you know you're being cared for.

TITHING AND GIVING TO GOD

Family Motto

"Tithe and thrive."

Bible Stories

Abraham tithes a tenth to Melchizedek (Genesis 14:8-24); Jacob's dream (Genesis 28:10-22).

We can explain to our kids that both Abraham and Jacob gave a tithe to God because they knew God had provided them with everything they had. To thank Him they gave back a tenth (tithe).

Faith Story

A good faith story would be how God first showed you about tithing (or perhaps someone you know).

Memory Verse

"Honor the Lord with your wealth, with the firstfruits of all your crops; then your barns will be filled to overflowing, and your vats will brim over with new wine" (Proverbs 3:9-10).

Definition

The word *tithe* means one tenth, or ten cents out of a dollar, or one dollar out of ten dollars. It is also called the firstfruits because when God gives to us we give the first part of what we get back to Him (or the first dollar out of every ten) before we use the rest on other things.

We give this to God to show Him we believe He owns everything and He is the one looking after us. We don't have to give *only* a tenth but this is a good place to start. The main place God wants us to give our tithes is to the church we attend. That's the way churches have money enough to do His work. All the people who go to that church give God's tenth to it and God lets the church leaders use it. Our tithes also can be used by the church to help people in need.

Tips

1. We should let our kids see us tithe in a way they understand. One expert, when his children were smaller, wrote the tithe check and cashed it. Before leaving for church on Sunday morning, while having breakfast with the kids, they all filled their offering envelopes. The kids didn't know what a check was, but seeing bunches of money stuffed into the offering envelopes left a lasting impression.

2. We can start children tithing as soon as they can divide it easily into their budget categories. This way they can separate their tithe instantly. We should encourage them to put their tithe aside, ready to give, before doing anything else with their money.

3. It is not helpful to just give kids a quarter to put in the offering plate. This has bad side effects. If they see the plate coming and drop a quarter in, they have no concept of giving. They didn't earn it; it had no cost to them.

4. Let's not forget to track the results of our kids' giving for them. When we see God's blessing or provision on our kids or on our family finances, no matter how small the miracle seems, we can talk about it. We can point it out to them and explain that we feel it is God blessing us and taking care of us.

5. We should explain to our kids what their money is used for at the church but without putting too much emphasis on it. The most important thing is that our children understand they are giving to God.

Many churches take an offering in Sunday school classes or children's church. Some go further by supplying envelopes for the kids to write their names and amounts on, and some even supply a receipt at the end of the year with the child's total on it. Some churches have special projects, like supporting a child from a developing country, and the children give their money toward that project.

We can suggest ideas like these to the leaders at our churches who are in charge of the children's area. These things really help kids understand and get excited about giving to the church. If our church doesn't do this, we can track it for our kids ourselves. Then we can make out a mock receipt for them when we get ours.

Activities

Have a special giving supper!

Every time you and your children give, you should pray a celebration prayer, thanking God for His provision, blessing, and care. Also, thank Him for the church He has let you be a part of and for the opportunity to give to Him and help the church at the same time. An ideal time for this is in the car before you leave for church: pray for God to teach you, change you, and help you to be a blessing to others in your church.

In addition, every once in a while (you might find a way to do it each week or once a month), just before you give your tithe, have a *special giving supper:* you choose a special meal, a great dessert the family loves, and make an evening everyone looks forward to. The purpose of the evening is to celebrate God's goodness. Spend a bit more time in your prayer thanking God for everything He has given you (including the intangibles). Everyone presents their tithes to God and says thanks for the wonderful blessings He's given them. Put the tithe on the center of the table and have a party atmosphere.

What this does is clearly demonstrate the attitude and thankfulness in which we are to give, and it reinforces the reasons for giving. Do whatever it takes for your kids to feel this is a special dinner: simple decorations, using the good dishes, candlelight, or whatever you wish. You also could give the kids turns picking their favorite menu.

Note: We should allow our young teenage children the opportunity to make the decision to give or not give so they can learn while they are still at home. If we have taught them the reasons, gotten them excited about following this principle, and shown them God's hand of blessing on their lives and on the family, we'll find the choice will be easy for them. We not only have shown them where to bury their treasure, but we've helped their hearts to follow.

Pointers

For parents who haven't started to tithe yet, a great activity would be to grow in God's grace in this area together with your children. You can talk to your kids about what you've learned and have a giving supper to launch the whole family into this commitment.

In all of this, we need to be sure we show and teach our kids about God's purpose for the local church. We give to God. One of the things God has given us responsibility for is supporting our church. Why? Because church is an important part of God's plan and He wants us to be there, learn and grow there, get involved there, and help and support it with our finances.

Kids need to be reminded why we do things. Then they can grow in understanding and find ways to get excited about God's purposes instead of just growing tired of the ritual.

BEING GENEROUS
IN GIVING TO OTHERS

Family Motto

"We live to give."

Bible Story

The good Samaritan (Luke 10:25-37).

Some people get caught up in trying to decipher, define, and separate tithing from giving and offerings—and even second and third tithes. We chose the story of the good Samaritan and the memory verse that talks about a cheerful giver because of the need to teach our kids a different focus. We should talk to our kids about having a giving attitude. If we truly believe God takes care of us, we should have no fear of cheerfully meeting the needs of others.

The story of the good Samaritan helps us to realize how we are to joyfully respond to those who need our help. If we teach our kids to be generous, compassionate, and willing to give, their question when they're older won't be, "How can I help when I don't have enough time and resources?" It will be, "God, please give me the wisdom and resources to help."

Faith Story

Tell your children about a time God had you sacrifice some of your wants and/or desires to meet someone else's needs. Tell them how the person responded and how that made you feel.

Memory Verse

"Remember this: Whoever sows sparingly will also reap sparingly, and whoever sows generously will also reap generously. Each man should give what he has decided in his heart to give, not reluctantly or under compulsion, for God loves a cheerful giver" (2 Corinthians 9:6,7).

Definition

Generosity is caring about other people's needs as well as our own. We are generous when we give up some of our wants and desires in order to help someone else with a need. We can do this cheerfully when we remember that God owns everything and that

He will take care of us.

An *offering* is money we give above our tithes. Sometimes this is for a collection taken by our church for a specific reason, like helping a missionary. Offerings also can be money we give to other ministries that aren't part of our church. God doesn't expect us to give every time someone asks for money, but He does always want us to be willing. We can pray and ask God for wisdom and direction when we have a chance to give an offering. He'll help us know what to give and to whom.

Tips

1. If our children are quite young or just being introduced to the idea of giving, we shouldn't load them down all at once with tithing, offerings, giving to others, and giving to the poor. We can start with tithing and work slowly from there.

2. Work on the attitude first. When giving is enjoyable and is seen as a good time by our kids, then we can start to expand the opportunities.

3. It's important to find new, fun projects and ways of giving. Christmastime provides many opportunities and projects to get involved with our kids.

4. We can pray together with our kids and ask God to give us opportunities to give—and not just our money, but our time, our care, or perhaps something our family has an abundance of.

Activities

A few activities for teaching this principle have been mentioned already.

• As a family project, sponsor a child through one of the organizations that give to needy children, but don't just pay the monthly payment yourself; let your kids contribute from their money as well. Collect the money, choose the agency, send the money, and read the response letters together as a family. Then you can pray together for your sponsored child.

• Take on a project that helps someone close to home, even a family member. Perhaps you might give up a Saturday and paint a senior citizen's fence, do something for a widow, or help a single mother. Another way to give is by visiting someone in a hospital or nursing home who is lonely. You want to teach your kids to look for ways to help others.

• If an offering is announced that you feel you should give to, pray as a family for ways of earning extra money that week and work together to make a contribution to that offering.

Note: Although giving and helping should be part of our lives, they shouldn't *become* our lives. If we spend too much time doing this, our kids' enthusiasm will wane and they will start to feel less cheerful. They might even begin to feel rather like slaves for hire, being dragged around by their parents. Everything in moderation. Keep it fun. Keep it in balance with the other parts of life. Look for variety, and look for opportunities that the family will get excited about.

Pointers

Look for the opportunity to bring this one closer to home. We want to establish in our children the attitude of giving and providing the needs of others.

The place to start is by helping them give to their brothers and sisters at home and to cheerfully contribute to the family's well-being. Who gets that last cookie? We want a response such as, "My younger brother should get it; these are his favorite." When they are asked by one of their siblings if they can borrow something, do they respond with a cheerful yes or an automatic no? We want to help our children adopt the "we live to give" motto every day and in everything. (Let's see if we can replace the word "no" in our family with the words "we live to give.")

We can make a commitment to our kids that we, as parents, will live by this motto too. This might mean we will consider their requests more carefully. We may be inconvenienced more often, but in finding a way to say yes we will help establish a live-to-give attitude in our children.

Once we have taught and established these four foundational principles in our children and they are active in doing them, we are well on our way to the goal of God-centered, confident, and financially equipped children

Things Inward

*I*f our children's treasures are in the right place, their hearts will be in the right place. Part of accomplishing this is to develop healthy attitudes and the outward actions that accompany those. Now we come to the practical teaching of the outworking of inner-heart attitudes.

CONTENTMENT

Family Motto

"Happy with God's gift—plenty or thrift."

Bible Story

Jesus' secrets for being content (Read about the temptation of Jesus, Matthew 4:1-11). Jesus had three secrets to being content.

Temptation #1: Do things your way and take care of yourself.

Jesus's Secret #1: Obey God, follow His principles and let Him take care of you.

Temptation #2: Get what you want, do what you want, God will help you.

Jesus' Secret #2: Trust God, let Him do things His way in His time in your life.

Temptation #3: Go after all the things this world has to offer.

Jesus' Secret #3: Serve and follow God. Don't go after the things that are made; go after and serve the Maker.

Read to your children from Matthew. *"But seek first his kingdom and his righteousness, and all these things will be given to you as well"* (Matthew 6:33). We can't go after the world and what it offers and serve God at the same time. But if we serve and follow God, He will always take care of us.

Faith Story

Tell your kids of a time you were tempted to go after the almighty dollar and compromise God's principles, your priorities, or your calling. Then tell them how God confirmed your right decision or taught you through your wrong choice.

Memory Verse

"Keep your lives from the love of money and be content with what you have, because God has said, 'Never will I leave you; never will I forsake you'" (Hebrews 13:5).

Definition

Contentment is being at peace because we trust God, no matter what our financial or life situations are. It doesn't matter what's going on if we know God is in control. Sometimes contentment comes from knowing God is taking care of us and changing things for the better. But it also means learning to be satisfied with what God has given us and what He is asking us to do. The biggest reason being content is important is so that, like Jesus in His temptation, we will follow God and not things. Contentment is one of the secrets to a happy life. In contrast, things never bring happiness.

Tips

1. It's easy to use the little things in family life to teach contentment. Society all around us says, "More!" "Bigger!" "Best!" The Bible calls these indulgence, greed, pride. When a squabble breaks out about who got more ice cream, it's simple to show our kids how not being content has just ruined the pleasure of the experience. We can help them understand what it is to be content even with the smallest desires.

2. After our children understand the difference between *needs, wants,* and *desires,* we can teach them how to talk to God about them. They also can tell Him they are willing to have what He knows is best, because they trust Him.

3. We want to remind our kids about stewardship and that even though they may be saving a part of their income for a desire God may prompt them to meet someone else's need with that money.

Note: Be careful! As parents overseeing our children's savings and finances, we may be tempted to say, "No, you can't give away the money you're saving for a new bike. You need the bike next month." It's better to keep quiet and encourage obedience and sacrificial giving. And we can remind ourselves that God isn't limited to our children's savings if they really need bikes right away.

Activities

Play "identi-scam."

A good opportunity to talk about contentment is when television commercials come on. Helping your children recognize how advertising ploys tempt them to violate God's principles is a great teaching opportunity. It's important to make it fun, though. Call it "identi-scam" and ask your kids to identify how the advertiser is trying to manipulate them. They will really sink their teeth into this.

Pointers

We should keep looking for other opportunities to teach and transfer the principle of contentment. When an opportunity to get a part in a play, go on a camping trip, or some other event children really desire comes up, we can help them apply contentment to the situation. We might have them pray and submit their desires to God, which will again affirm their trust.

In later years, we can help them apply contentment when they want to go to a particular school or get married. Our kids will learn that any time they really want something it is an opportunity to apply the principle of contentment.

HONESTY

Family Motto

"Honesty is our **only** policy!"

Bible Story

Dishonest Gehazi (2 Kings 5).

We should point out two things about this story. First, Gehazi didn't think what he did was wrong; he justified himself. However, it's not us who decides right from wrong; it is God. God didn't want Elisha and Gehazi to take Naaman's gifts. (Gehazi knew that or he wouldn't have lied about it.) It wouldn't have been wrong if God had said it was okay. Dishonesty is disobeying God.

Draw attention to Elisha's comment in verse 26. Gehazi had removed his focus from God and moved it onto things. That caused him to be dishonest. When we are honest, we show we trust God.

Also, we can read about Ananias and Sapphira in Acts 5:1-11. This story accurately demonstrates how God feels about dishonesty.

Faith Story

Tell about a time when you were tempted to be dishonest. If you gave in to the temptation, you can explain the result. If you were able to resist it, you can share with your children how it worked out for you.

Memory Verse

"He whose walk is upright fears the Lord, but he whose ways are devious despises him" (Proverbs 14:2).

Definition

Honesty is a characteristic of God. He is honest. The Bible says God is Truth and He cannot lie. Honesty means always bringing out the whole truth in what we do and say. God made everything to work best with honesty: relationships, finances, our word—everything. When we choose honesty, no matter what, we show that we trust God. He will take care of us. In finances, honesty isn't just not lying or cheating; it's being sure we are fair.

Tips

This principle is especially important for us to model for our kids. The level of our honesty or dishonesty in everything—from not letting our spouse know we bought the kids ice cream, all the way to cheating on our income tax—will be seen, learned, and copied. We live in a society of relative truth. As a result, many dishonest things are justified. We need to raise the standard. Dishonesty does not work, it stops God's blessing. Honesty lines up with God and everything He made. It works. We need to demonstrate it to our kids.

Activity

Play "Proverbial Charades."

Write each of these verses from the NIV on a separate piece of paper.

"The man of integrity walks securely, but he who takes crooked paths will be found out" (Proverbs 10:9).

"The integrity of the upright guides them, but the unfaithful are destroyed by their duplicity" (Proverbs 11:3).

"The plans of the righteous are just, but the advice of the wicked is deceitful" (Proverbs 12:5).

"He whose walk is upright fears the Lord, but he whose ways are devious despises him" (Proverbs 14:2).

"A good name is more desirable than great riches; to be esteemed is better than silver or gold" (Proverbs 2:1).

"Better a poor man whose walk is blameless than a rich man whose ways are perverse" (Proverbs 28:6).

"He who conceals his sins does not prosper, but whoever confesses and renounces them finds mercy" (Proverbs 28:13).

Put the pieces of paper in a hat, a bag, a bowl, or a box. You can play this individually, or parents may want to team up with younger children. The first person closes his or her eyes and picks up a piece of paper. He or she then has to act out that proverb for the whole family.

This game will automatically create the opportunity for discussion. Everyone will want to talk about how the charade represented the proverb (or not). This leads to discussion on the meaning of the verse. However, it's better not to force such a discussion; just let it happen.

Note: Limiting the time to guess the proverb will add excitement to the game.

Pointers

This pointer is rather simple. It's easy to see how learning honesty can benefit every other area of a child's life. We need to be sure this one is emphasized early on in our families. Children who learn to return the extra coins the vending machine gave them likely won't be dishonest in any other decision.

DILIGENCE

Family Motto

"Don't just do it. Do it right, do it quickly, and do it well!"

An article in the *Washington Times* says new job seekers are out of touch with reality. They want too much money. They are unwilling to train in an apprenticeship. They won't start at the bottom and work their way up the corporate ladder. The article states, "They display an attitude of superiority—completely unrelated to what they have to offer."

The self-esteem programs in public schools are backfiring. We have kids who feel great about themselves but who aren't willing to work.

Teaching a work ethic today is so important because the something-for-nothing, I-deserve-it, and get-rich-quick mentalities put forward by and entrenched in our culture teach the opposite.

Bible Story

Joseph the diligent (Genesis 39-41).

Read the story of Joseph and tell it to the kids in your own words. Show the children how God took Joseph from running a house to running a prison to running a country to running the food supply of the known world. God was able to do this for Joseph because of God's three-step work-ethic plan.

1. Joseph worked hard even when he was unjustly sold as a slave, because he worked like he was working for God, not for men. His good work was noticed by his master.

2. Because Joseph worked for God, he worked diligently and did his job with excellence. Then God was able to bless his work and reward him.

3. Next, Joseph's masters saw not only that Joseph was a great worker but that everything went well when he was in charge. As a result they promoted him. This was God's plan. (It's God who pro-

motes people, not men. When we work for Him instead of other people, things start to happen.)

God's Three-Step Work-Ethic Plan

1. We work hard, with excellence, because we are working for God—not for other people.

2. God rewards our hard and excellent work with His blessing.

3. God is able to promote us.

Memory Verse

"Whatever you do, work at it with all your heart, as working for the Lord, not for men" (Colossians 3:23).

Definition

Biblical *diligence* is doing everything we do for God and doing our very best. We are stewards of our lives, our work, our things, and everything else. If God were standing beside us and asked us to sweep the kitchen floor, would we miss a corner? Would we do it slowly and lazily? No! We need to learn to work hard, do a job really well and with excellence, concentrate to get the job done quickly, and do more than what is expected of us—all because we are working for God.

Diligence starts with the attitude in our hearts, then it works outward as we do the very best job we know how to do. If we are trying to please God and realize He is the one who is in charge of our lives—He is the one who promotes or demotes us—then it's easier to have a better attitude about other things. First, we may be doing a job we don't really like, like Joseph being a slave or working in a prison. But if we realize God has us here for a reason, we can still work diligently for Him.

Second, we may have to start in the work force for a wage that isn't desirable. However, we aren't working for a wage. We are working for God. He will take care of us when we work for Him, and He will help us get the promotion or raise when the time is right.

Tips

1. It's important to always have our kids watch us do a job at least once before we ask them to do it on their own. The second time we should be there with them, helping them and encouraging them—but not nagging. We shouldn't be surprised when they do it slowly and sloppily to start with. We need to train them. It's much more helpful to make the task joyful, play a bit, and have some fun in the process, encourage them, and praise them when they get it right. If they do it wrong again, we simply offer to show them a second time how it's done.

2. With each job we train our kids to do, we should train them in diligence and the work ethic. We can remind them they are working for the best boss possible: God. He has no limits on His bonus system; it even extends into eternity. We should teach them that working hard means putting a lot of energy into something, while concentrating on what we're doing and how we've been taught to do it. We should teach them how to work quickly, always trying to pick up their speed once they are better at the job. (This comes naturally when they're playing video games!) Also, we must teach them to do the job well and double-check the end product or result, making sure they've been absolutely thorough. We also want to encourage them to see if there is something they can do that is a little more than what is expected.

Activities

Make a "job board."

Post a job board for the purpose of teaching your kids about individual effort for remuneration and helping them to learn that the quality of the job they do directly affects their short-term reward and long-term reputation. A piece of cardboard about 12" x 18" with the words "Quality Labor Required" on the top is recommended. Have a pad of post-it notes handy. It should be easy to find jobs for your kids that are beyond the usual cleaning up after themselves and doing their family share. Write the job on a post-it-note with the amount it will pay when the job is well done. For example: clean out refrigerator - $3.00, clean garage - $6.00, wash and vacuum car - $4.00.

On the bottom of the job board, write the "Terms of Employment":

- Every job must be inspected before payment is made.
- No job partially done will receive payment.
- Pray before choosing jobs. Be sure you don't take on more than you can do.
- All jobs must be done diligently. This means to work hard, do quickly, and do well.
- All regular chores must be completed before taking a job from the job board.
- Management reserves the right not to pay for slack, slow, or sloppy work. Management also reserves the right to pay bonuses for jobs that are well done.

It's best not to pay the kids by the hour. Even working for an hour is a hard thing for younger kids to grasp. It's better to pay them by the job. This also helps establish money as a means of exchange. The quicker they get the job done, the more valuable their time is. We want to help them see this. Once we start the job board, we should keep it going and keep the rules. If we bend the rules we've established, we will have defeated the job board's purpose.

With kids in different age groups that require different levels of work, when you post the job you may need to put on the post-its an age range for the person required. For example:

"Sweep the porch - $1.00.

Skills required - Must be between 6 and 7 and good with a broom."

Pointers

Diligence is a principle that needs to be applied to school work, relationships, financial planning, devotional lives—even personal grooming. Once children have learned how to work hard, quickly, and well, instead of being slack, slow, and sloppy, they can apply that to every area of their lives.

Financial Management

*I*n previous chapters we dealt with the financial principles that more readily deal with heart and attitude issues.
In this chapter and the next we want to continue the practical helps, tips, ideas, and resources for teaching the outworking
of all we've learned. In this chapter we will deal with the areas of
organizing and planning our finances.

LONG-TERM
FINANCIAL PLANNING

Family Motto

"Put a plan in His hands!"

Bible Story

God has a plan for you! (Psalm 139:1-18).

"Your eyes saw my unformed body. All the days ordained for me were written in your book before one of them came to be" (Psalm 139:16).

It's important to talk to children about God knowing everything. He knows what is happening right now everywhere. He knows what is about to happen and everything that will happen in the future. God has a plan for our lives. He knows us better than we know ourselves. When we give our lives to Him and trust Him for wisdom and direction, our lives are where they were created to be: in God's hands.

Faith Story
Tell how God revealed His plan for part of your life.

Memory Verse
"Trust in the Lord with all your heart and lean not on your own understanding; in all your ways acknowledge him, and he will make your paths straight" (Proverbs 3:5-6).

Definition
Long-term financial planning is drawing a map of where we are and where we want to go, and how we will get there. The plan looks at three things: what we believe God has for us, how we will prepare for that thing, and the money needed for the preparation and plan.

We never want to make plans that leave God out. We should talk to God about everything. He loves us and wants the best for us. What we want is to have our financial plan match God's plan for us. The reason we plan is to make sure we are being good stewards.

We need to see if we are doing what we need to do to get where God wants us to go. It's like being in a car and wanting to go somewhere specific. Once we know where we want to go, we check a map to see if the road we're on and the direction we're going will get us there. Remember, though, that God doesn't show us everything. Our "maps" will need regular prayer and adjusting as we go.

Tips

1. It is important to model this concept with our children. We can talk with them about where we believe God is taking us and update them on the plans and their stage of fulfillment. We're referring not just to our ultimate life goals but to smaller goals as well. The same process and principles apply.

2. Obviously, the older our children get the more detailed and accurate their plans will become. We don't need to worry, though, about starting them young and showing them simple plans, each with different goals (dentist, fire fighter, police officer, ballerina, nurse—all the regulars). This process can be used to help them to learn how to plan, keep them open to God's plan, and begin to learn the concept of preparation: what it takes to get there.

Activity

Make a "financial picture map."

For younger kids, this may involve the following steps. Get out the scissors, glue, pencils, crayons, old magazines and newspapers, and a sheet of paper or cardboard for each child.

Once you're all set, pray a simple prayer, affirming that God has a plan for each person's life and asking Him for wisdom and direction. Then each child says what he or she thinks God might want that child to do when he or she is older. (This gets the same result as asking, "What do you want to be when you grow up?" but the recommended phrasing begins to plant the right seeds.)

Find or draw pictures that represent the children's answers and put them on one corner of the paper. For example, if they said they think God wants them to be dentists or doctors, find pictures of a dentist, a set of teeth, a tube of toothpaste, or a doctor's office from an ad. Now, write "Dr. (the child's name)" under the pictures. As you are doing this, talk to the child about what a dentist (or doctor) does. Next, draw or find pictures you don't mind gluing down of the children, and put them in the other corner of the paper.

Find pictures that go in the center of the page that represent the steps needed to achieve the careers: university, college, savings account, trade school, medical school, part-time jobs, sacks of money, numbers representing years, and so on.

The older the child is the more complicated it can be. For the youngest kids, the center might just be a school, a bank, or an airplane. For older kids, you can do this with paper and words. You might use circles with each major career step written in them joined together by lines. Then you can add another set of corresponding circles that contain the financial details. This might involve doing some research or even interviewing someone in his or her chosen profession to discover what are the best steps to follow. After interviewing someone about what the job entails, the child might decide that it isn't what he or she wanted after all. We need to encourage our children to explore possibilities and then find out what it takes to get there.

It's important not to push your kids beyond what they can grasp at the time. After doing this a few times, they will want to add and do more. For teenage kids, their financial maps should begin to line up with their budgets. (See Budgeting, this section.)

Pointers

The three most important elements of career planning can be reinforced in the youngest of children.

1. God has a plan for you.

2. God has given you unique gifts that match His plan for you.

3. God will guide and direct you as you pray for His wisdom and direction.

Any Christian career planner will tell you that establishing these three things is most of the battle. If a youth walks in convinced of these three elements, the rest is relatively simple. When we as parents teach these three basics to our children and then take them to the planning stage, we have given them the foundation for making every educational and career decision they will ever have to make. (There are books listed in the Appendix on career planning.)

BUDGETING

Family Motto
"Pray, plan, and write it out; follow it without a doubt."

Bible Story
Gideon's budget (Judges 6-7). (Read this to your kids if they are older. If you have younger children, read it and retell it, or read the story to them out of a Bible storybook.)

You may think calling this story Gideon's budget is a bit of a stretch, but think of the allegory. We can explain to our kids that Gideon gathered a large number of men for his army. God let him know he didn't need that many to get the job done. God pared back Gideon's army to a mere 300 men, then He gave Gideon wisdom so he could defeat the massive army of his enemy with just those men—with God's help of course.

We can let our kids know that when it comes to money we often think, like Gideon's enemy, that what we need is a lot. But the principle is, it's not how much we have that matters, it's following God's principles and asking for His wisdom. Then, as we're obedient and trust Him, He will help so that we win—or have enough. God doesn't necessarily give us more. He helps us get the most out of what we have.

One particular day while I (Larry) was counseling, three couples came to see me.

Couple #1 I asked, "What's the problem?" They responded by stating, "We don't have enough money. We can't live on what we make." Together we examined their income and expenses (they made $18,000 and needed $25,000). It seemed clear that there was no way they could live on what they were making. They were right. I sent them away while I considered their problem.

Couple #2 An hour or two later a second couple came in. Asking the same question, "What's the problem?" I received the same response, "We don't have enough money" (they made $38,000 and needed $55,000). Again, it seemed clear that they were correct; they could not live on what they were making.

Couple #3 A third couple came in. I again asked, "What's the problem?" They replied, "We don't have enough money" (this couple made $75,000 but needed $95,000). They could not live on what they were making.

It became clear that the amount of money each couple made was not the real problem. The issue was how they used the money they had.

Faith Story

Tell your kids a story about how you learned to budget and the benefits it brought.

Memory Verse

"The Lord said to Gideon, 'With the three hundred men that lapped I will save you and give the Midianites into your hands. Let all the other men go, each to his own place'" (Judges 7:7).

Note: This memory verse will only work and serve as a reminder for our kids if we read the story and do the activity.

Definition

We *budget* when we write down a plan for what we are going to do with our money.

The first step in a Christian's budget should be to figure the amount of the tithe. Other items in the budget include taxes, bills and expenses, spending money, and savings. The two basic steps to a budget are exactly what our motto says.

1. Pray, plan, and write down the plan.
2. Follow the plan.

Tips & Activities

As soon as kids are old enough to understand what money is and to receive it and spend it, they are ready for a pre-budget. The idea is to take the kids gradually from a pre-budget to a full fifteen-category budget by the time they live on their own. We will suggest at least two other stages between pre-budget and budget, but it's important to expand, contract, or alter these to fit our own kids' expenditures.

Pre-budget (Ages 3-8)

The Giving Bank (see the Appendix for more information) is the perfect tool for the pre-budget. It is a bank that is divided into three connected storage containers: one for "giving," one for "saving," and one for "spending." The three categories are contributed to according to two levels of pre-budget. Three-, four- and five-year-olds should be given three coins (or three bills) and instructed to put one in each container: one for God (church), one for saving (bank), and one to spend (store).

Around 6 or 7 years of age our kids should be given percentages. Ten percent of their money goes to tithing, 50 percent to savings, and 40 percent to spending. We need to be sure our kids are given their money so they can divide it easily (for example, $2, $4, $6). We will have to help them in the process at first.

The distribution of money should be as follows: "dump and give," "dip and spend," "want and save." "Dump and give" happens on Sunday morning when we help them dump their money out of the giving compartment and give it to the church. "Dip and spend" happens when money is needed. "Want and save" stays in the bank for now.

At the pre-budget stage the only thing that needs to be written down is the savings or "want and save" goal. We should help the child choose something that won't take too long to save for but represents something more expensive and special than what he or she can get with his or her "dip and spend" money.

Write whatever your children are saving for on post-it notes and stick them on the bank. Or find pictures of the items and stick those on the bank. We want to have our kids stick to this goal; it's their first experience with making a budget and sticking to it. (If you don't have a *Giving Bank*, three envelopes or separate marked containers will work.)

Mini-budget (Ages 9-12)

A mini-budget can still be housed in the *Giving Bank*, but a little more budgeting or writing down is now required. It will be necessary to get our kids in this age group a little notebook to go along with their banks. The notebook starts to approximate a bank book and budget ledger.

An important point to teach them is, just because the container has a certain amount of money in it, they cannot necessarily spend it all on one thing. That money has different purposes according to the plan, which at this point will consist of four categories.

Giving: 10 percent

Saving-a-little: 25 percent (short-term savings)

Saving-a-lot: 25 percent (long-term savings)

Spending: 40 percent

The two categories of "saving-a-little" and "saving-a-lot" replace the "want and save" category of the pre-budget. But both still get saved in the same "saving" section of the bank.

We suggest their notebook look like the following.

Page 1 In their notebook we should have them write on the first page the four budget categories with their percentages.

Page 2 Top—our motto, the budget two-step:

1. Pray, plan, and write it out.

2. Follow it without a doubt.

Middle—picture of the item (optional).

Bottom—"Saving-a-little." We can explain that this is for a short-term plan. (Not all savings should be allocated before it's saved, but right now we are trying to teach them to save and plan for what they want and desire. The rest will come later.)

Have the children think of something they want that would probably take three to six weeks to save for (help them figure this out). Have them write what they decide on and what it will cost. If they don't know what it will cost, the next step is to help them find out.

Page 3 "Saving-a-little Diary"

Each time they put money into their savings bank, they should write on this page how much goes toward this goal.

Page 4 Top—Rewrite the motto.

Middle—Picture the item (optional).

Bottom—"Saving-a-lot." They should have a goal that will take three to six months to reach. They should write how much their goals will cost. (After our kids save successfully a few times and as they get older, we can allow them to save for things that will take longer. For example: "Saving-a-little," 2-to-3 month goal; "Saving-a-lot," up to a year goal.)

Page 5 "Saving-a-lot Diary"

Each time they put money in their savings bank, they should write how much goes toward this goal.

The important thing in the mini-budget is to keep short the time periods the kids are saving, to start with, so that they can reach their goals quickly and get excited about the process. When they reach their goals we can get excited with them. It will be helpful to praise them for saving and to go through the spending procedure with them right away. If we delay the purchase—the gratification and pay-off for all their hard work—they might lose some of the motivation toward saving we're trying to build in them.

In the mini-budget, giving should still be "dump and give" and spending should still be "dip and spend." We can let them spend this money however they wish (in keeping with family dietary and media content rules, of course).

Remember, when the spending money is gone, it's gone. We don't supplement it in any of these budgets. That would defeat the purpose. We are training our children to physically understand the value of their money as they budget it. Bailing them out gives the wrong message.

Teen-budget
(Ages 13 until flying lessons—just before they leave the nest)

We suggest adding two other budget categories to the teen budget to help better prepare them for all-out budgeting.

1. Giving	10 percent
2. Community "taxes"	5 percent
3. Short-term savings	25 percent
4. Long-term savings	25 percent
5. Expenses	10 percent
6. Spending	25 percent

First, let's deal with the functional systems. Obviously, the *Giving Bank* won't work anymore. It's time to open checking and savings accounts. At this stage, our kids don't need games, piggy banks, or activities that are allegories for functional financial systems. They need to start learning how these systems actually work.

Take the children to the bank and have them talk to the teller and open a savings account and a checking account. Be sure they ask all the right questions and the teller adequately explains how things work.

Perhaps you wonder, "Why two accounts? Shouldn't we start simply, with only one?" Starting with two accounts continues the consistent message: "It's not all one spending source." Teach your children how to reconcile their bank statements and how to keep a check register. Also, as they get older, make any and all payments due to them by check for allowances and job board earnings. Don't put the spend-the-cash-before-it's-in-the-bank temptation in front of them. And, again, pay them regularly.

This whole move to banking can be approached with the welcome-to-adulthood parental motivation method. In other words, we tell them that after their 13th birthday they get to have their own bank accounts and checkbooks. We want to get them excited about the getting-older-and-getting-more-important-responsibilities process. We don't need to explain it all in one day. It's okay to pace ourselves. The point is to get started and keep our kids motivated and asking questions. We must not push them to boredom or we'll be pushing the process backward, not forward.

Discipline does play a role in any training process, but if we approach it right (using the principles of approach discussed earlier) we can cut down on the need. Plus, one of the reasons for starting early is so that there is no emergency deadline requiring our kids to have this all down pat right away. Remember how long it took us to get these things right?

When we talk about learning systems, the decision, "to allow a credit card or not to allow a credit card—and when" comes up. We will offer suggestions in chapter 11 in the "Debt and Credit" section.

Let's deal with the two added categories in the teen budget.

Community "Taxes"

The saying goes, "There are two things in life that are certain: death and taxes." If our kids know Jesus, we've prepared them for the biggest of the two. Now it's time to prepare them for taxes. The idea is that if we teach our kids to have a good attitude toward taxes when they are young we better prepare them for life. If we wait until the tax system starts eliminating money without warning, they could become disgruntled with the system.

Jesus said, "*Give to Caesar what is Caesar's, and to God what is God's*" (Matthew 22:21). We can read the story surrounding this verse with our kids when they add this category to their budgets. We should explain the good, practical things around us we take for granted that are paid for by taxes. It's debt financing and government handouts that have brought us to where we are—not the concept of community betterment through community contribution: taxes. So, what do we do with the money?

Suggestion We can set up a "community tax" box in our homes. We should contribute to it ourselves, perhaps matching what our kids put into it. This can be a box, an envelope, or a jar kept in the kitchen, marked "community tax." Later we can decide as a family how this money is to be spent. It should be spent on something that mutually benefits the whole family. It could be a long-term goal, like a barbecue grill or a computer. It could be a more immediate goal, like buying a new video for the family each month.

If a complaint arises among our taxpayers about their younger sibling citizens who are not paying taxes, this is a good time to explain how taxation works. Also, we need to be careful not to use this fund for something that doesn't benefit our kids.

Expenses

Again, the idea behind the growing complexity of our kids' budgets is to lead them gradually into establishing a full budget when they leave home, introducing a few more basic concepts with each new level.

Perhaps the largest budget category in adult life is regular bills and expenses. We suggest that teens be introduced to this category, starting with 10 percent of their income. We can figure what approximately 10 percent of our teen's total income is. (Allowance plus an average earned from the job board plus any regular or averageable outside income.)

Next, help them find an expense that needs to be paid on a regular basis that approximately equals that amount. This could be lessons of some sort, monthly dues at the community center, a telephone of their own (billed directly to them). Or it could be several less expensive items, such as a subscription to a Christian magazine and the extra monthly cost for the call-waiting option on the family phone, (so they can talk to their friends without interrupting the flow of communication to the rest of the household). The key is to match the expense with our kids by finding something they are interested in.

When our kids first start getting their bills, we will need to work with them in order to ensure they get into the habit of keeping their paperwork in order and paying their bills on time.

We should have them find a special place, such as a desk drawer, for their financial paperwork. We need to make sure they keep everything—checkbook, bankbook, bank statement, receipts, bills, expense contracts, the budget book, and so forth—in this one place.

Note: This expense category should not go to the payment of a debt as a result of buying something over time with payments. That would invert the save-then-spend policy we are trying to teach them and would put them on the world's track of buy-then-pay.

Our kids on the teen-budget will need to keep budget books. We will need to help them set up the budget books. (Loose-leaf binders with pockets are a good idea.)

Page 1 Write the budget two-step (our motto):

1. Pray, plan, and write it out.
2. Follow it without a doubt.

Page 2 Write their six budget categories and their percentages.

Page 3 In a giving record write each payment and when they gave it. It's easy for kids to forget whether they gave or not this month when they first move away from dump-and-give. This page should also record extra giving, helping others, helping the needy, or special offerings. They can write out family "faith projects" here too. (At this stage of budgeting, extra giving should first of all come out of spending, to help demonstrate the immediate sacrifice needed to follow God and give. If the giving goal is greater, we should help them adjust their short-term savings goals. Or we could even make meeting a certain need one of their short-term goals.)

Page 4 Write what the family has decided to spend the community tax money on and keep a record of their payments. These payments should be made in cash so there won't be an extra accounting burden for the family administrator.

Page 5 Short-term savings: This is the same as in the mini-budget, except with an average three- to six-month goal. (Sometimes a shorter term is okay but we shouldn't let them always set shorter goals.)

Page 6 Long-term savings: The kids should begin to line up this category with their "financial plan." For example, if they have prayed and set a plan to attend the university and saving a portion of the needed money is part of the means to the goal, then their long-term savings should go in that direction now. If they want to buy a computer for themselves, and it's not part of their long-term plan, this becomes a desire and they will need to save their short-term savings for a longer time in order to get it. Have them put a copy of their financial plan into the binder right beside their long-term savings so they can track them together.

Page 7 Expenses: Have the kids keep a record of the dates and amounts of their payments. These should be made by check. The payment contract or paperwork and each month's invoice or bill can be kept in the pocket of the binder.

Page 8 (the rest of the book) A general "What did I make and where did it go?" page should be done for each month. This should be as simple as money-in amounts from each source, total, and the amounts paid into each category. We can have them check the percentages and give themselves a tick mark for the correct amounts. (Or assess what went wrong and fix it.) The key is that their money-in should balance their money-out or money-allocated.

All of this might be simple for some kids and extremely difficult for others. We will need to assess when the right age is for children to move to the teen budget. It might be 11, or it could be 15. It would be better for them to be consistent on the mini-budget for a longer time than to start them on a system on which they will fail. You don't want them to be discouraged. Once they start it is crucial you don't demand and abandon! Work with them as long as it takes for them to get it. You don't want to do it *for* them but *with* them. They'll tell us if we stay too long; independence will speak once confidence is instilled.

Moving to a Full Budget

When it's getting close to the time for our kids to leave the nest, we will need to help them make the transition to a full budget. If you are not familiar with Christian Financial Concepts' fifteen-category budget, we recommend that you refer to some of the publications listed in the Appendix that are available from CFC. The percentages allocated for each category depend somewhat on the individual or family income. For your information, the categories are as follows:

1. Tithe	9. Food
2. Housing	10. Insurance
3. Automobile	11. Entertainment and Recreation
4. Debts	12. Savings
5. Clothing	13. Miscellaneous
6. Medical Expenses	14. Investments
7. School/Child Care	15. Unallocated Surplus.
8. Taxes	

At this point, if we haven't already done it, it is important to bring our kids in on our family budget and into the process of budgeting. We should let them see where we are spending our money. They will have to learn this. We can show them how much we spend on housing, cars, food, clothes, and the rest.

Note: We can let our kids manage our family finances for six months under our supervision. This is very much like a teenager learning to drive. No one simply hands over the car keys to a 16 year old with a "Good luck, see ya later." Instead, hours are spent training so the young person gets the feel of being behind the wheel.

It's the same with finances. Let your children "get the feel behind finances" before they leave home.

Also, we can buy them some financial planning workbooks and resources so they can continue learning on their own. Christian Financial Concepts has a variety of resources that can help with this.

Pointers

Once our teens are at the level of planning at which they can handle the elements of the budget without difficulty, we can add other planning elements to their lives. We can buy them day planners and help them keep their basic life schedules and perhaps also devotional diaries. We want to train them to budget not only their money but their time and energy. The skill of budgeting can be applied to every area of life.

Now we are ready to move on to the areas in which our children will be making the actual monetary transactions.

Transactions

By now our children have the foundations built solidly into their lives and are ready for the actual physical handling of money: putting what they've learned into practice.

SAVING AND INVESTING

Family Motto

"Do it today, invest and save, and the road to the future you will pave."

Bible Story

Joseph's saving plan (Genesis 41)

Read Genesis chapter 41 to your children. If they are younger, read it first and tell them the story or read it out of a Bible storybook.

We need to be careful that we teach our kids a balanced understanding and approach to saving. We can point out to them the wisdom God gave Joseph to know what to do. Joseph had been raised as Jacob's favorite son. If we read Jacob's employment history with his father-in-law Laban, we'll see how Joseph learned his work ethic and how he learned that wealth is built gradually, bit by bit, with God's wisdom and blessing.

Although Joseph, as a slave, had no money of his own, he managed every detail of Potiphar's house and, later, the prison. They both flourished. God had taught and prepared Joseph for the job he needed to do. This wasn't a one-time quick-fix Joseph came up with; it was the application of God's principles to a specific problem that God had revealed. Joseph applied the principles of saving for future needs by not consuming everything on hand, and he applied the principle of investing by storing up more than the Egyptians needed for the famine. In this way he was able to make huge returns by selling to the rest of the world.

We don't know what the future will bring, but God does. Fearing the future leads to hoarding; ignoring the future leads to excess. But following God's leading and applying His principles brings us to a balance.

Faith Story

Tell your kids of a time God was able to prepare you, through saving or investing, for something you could not foresee.

Memory Verse

"In the house of the wise are stores of choice food and oil, but a foolish man devours all he has" (Proverbs 21:20).

Definition

Saving is putting aside a planned amount of income each month. It is the way we get enough money to buy things that cost more than our budgets will let us spend in one month. Saving is also a way that God helps us get ready for the future He has planned for us: perhaps going to trade school, college, or university. Sometimes God uses savings to help us be ready for things in the future we don't know about or expect. Saving can also be a way for God to get us ready to help someone else.

Investing is taking a small, planned part of our income and buying something (like land), or putting it into a business or an account, with the goal of making more money. When the property becomes worth more, we make money. When the business or account makes money, so do we. God can use investing for all the same reasons as savings.

However, instead of getting a small amount of interest from the bank for keeping our money there, as we do with savings, investing wisely can help our money make more money faster. Investing is also different from saving because we possibly could lose our money if we invest poorly. Also, sometimes we have to leave our money in an investment for a certain length of time. So we should save first and invest wisely with only some of our savings.

Tips

1. We should give our kids savings goals as soon as possible. We can make the goals small to start with so they can see the rewards before they get impatient.

2. As soon as the kids meet their savings goals, it's important that we make a special point of quickly going with them to make their purchases. (By quickly, we don't mean to exclude the wise-buying process.)

3. When our kids are putting their savings in the bank we should teach them about interest. We can show them some simple numbers that illustrate how savings can grow because of compound interest over the years.

4. We should remind our kids to be flexible with their savings. God is the Master and we are the stewards. We may think we are

saving for one reason but the Master may have another purpose for that money—like meeting someone else's needs. This helps kids keep their eyes on God instead of getting them fixed too firmly on their savings. Our savings is not our provider. God is.

Activities

The Family Investment Program

1. There are several ways to teach kids about investing. One way now available is through a special investment fund for kids.

We recommend the together approach: letting your kids contribute to your investments. Show them what you are doing and why. For those of your kids on the teen budget you can provide photocopies of the main pieces of information and let them create an investment page in their budget binders. Your kids will get excited about doing this with you and will learn far more in the process.

If you don't have any investments, now might be the time to find one. Once you find one, pray about it and determine if it would be good for your family. Have a family meeting and ask everyone to assign a small part of their savings to the investment. You may have to save up before you have enough to get started. Keep everyone involved in praying for and managing the investment. (See the Appendix for a book on investing.)

Discuss with your kids the terms of the investment, its use, and the return it gets. It's important to give them the same terms. When it comes time to sell or cash in the investment, give your kids the same percentage of return on their investments that the entire investments earned. (To this end, be sure you invest wisely and not in something high risk. Kids should be taught to invest solidly. You can explain to them why you chose the investment you did.)

Note: It's important to be sure your kids keep investments in the proper perspective. If an investment works well and they get excited, the temptation might be to focus on that instead of what the money is for: living and giving.

2. Play the "Time Machine Saving Game." Take a shoe box and write "Time Machine" on it. When you are giving out allowances, explain to your kids how interest works: when you put your money in the bank, the bank uses it to make more money. Then the bank pays you interest for letting them use your money. After a while the interest makes your money grow.

Explain to your children that this box is a Time Machine. It works like a bank account, only faster. In one month the Time Machine will travel ten years into the future. Tell them they can choose any portion of their spendable allowance (excluding allocations for tithes, taxes, and other non-negotiables) and put it in this Time Machine for the month. Be sure to explain that this means they won't be able to use that money for the month. Explain that the Time Machine will take their money ten years into the future and earn ten years of interest. Don't calculate the interest for them. Let them decide on their own whether they want to play and how much they will put into the Time Machine.

Next month, when you are giving out allowances, show the kids what happened to their money. It has earned 10 percent interest, compounded for ten years. (A rough calculation for this can be to multiply the amount by 2.5—$1.00 becomes $2.50 in ten years.)

They probably will want to play the game again. You can explain that the Time Machine only works once for each child. If they want to play again, they can put their money in a bank account where it will earn interest at the normal rate.

The point is to impress on the children the benefit of saving, as opposed to borrowing. (You can explain the concept of paying interest as well. More on this under "Debt and Credit" in this section.)

Pointers

Show your kids through the hands-on practice of saving and

investing that every decision we make affects our future. Wisdom now, even though it may mean sacrifice, will result in greater future reward. God's system does not involve living *for* the moment. His system is living at peace and contentment *in* the moment and making right choices that will build for tomorrow.

This principle can be applied to larger peer pressure decisions and life temptations that will confront our kids. If they learn the principle and see the results of following it in the simple area of finances, more complex decisions, like saving oneself for one's marriage partner, are easier to understand and follow.

SPENDING

Family Motto
"Shop till you drop but don't spend till the end."

Bible Story
The son who spent like there was no tomorrow (Luke 15:11-32)

Read this passage to your kids. (Retelling the story in your own words or reading a Bible storybook version might be better for younger kids.) Then point out three things from this story about wrong spending.

1. We need to live as stewards, not for what money can buy.

2. The way we spend money shows things about ourselves. *"Where our treasure is, there will our heart be, also."* We need to spend our money on good things.

3. We need to spend our money wisely so we can also plan for the future: sacrifice now to build for tomorrow.

The son who was the foolish spender didn't want to do what his father wanted him to. He just wanted money and the things it could buy. The foolish spender spent his money on ungodly things, which proved even more that he didn't trust God. If he had trusted God he would have done what God said to do, not the opposite. And he spent all of his money, keeping nothing for the future.

God wants us to trust and obey Him and let Him care for us. Jesus said we couldn't serve God and money, because if we go after money and the things it can buy we put those things first, instead of God. We prove we trust God when we obey Him and follow His principles. So we prove we trust God when we sacrifice now, spend wisely, and save.

Faith Story

Tell your kids a story of when you were tempted to spend foolishly but made the right choice and how it worked out. Or perhaps tell how you made the wrong choice and learned from it.

Memory Verse

"After he had spent everything, there was a severe famine in that whole country, and he began to be in need" (Luke 15:14).

Definition

Spending is not the opposite of saving; it's the opposite of earning. Money is a means of exchange. You earn it and you spend it. In and out. Saving is keeping some of your spending ability for another time.

There is nothing wrong with spending money. We just need to be sure we are being wise stewards of how we spend it. Eventually we spend all of the money we earn, so knowing *how* to spend it is important. There are three general rules for spending.

1. We don't *have* to buy anything. We need to learn to follow God's wisdom and tell the difference between our needs, our wants, and our desires.

2. When we do spend our money we must spend it wisely. This means spending our money on things the Master approves of, making sure we get good value (good product and a good price).

3. We need to learn not to spend everything we have right

away. We can plan to spend a certain amount and then stick to our plan.

Tips

1. We don't want to leave our kids with the idea that spending is wrong and saving is right. Saving is just delayed spending. Even giving is spending our money on others. The goal is to discourage foolish spending and teach and encourage wise spending.

2. We should clearly separate money we spend on our kids from money they spend on themselves. Otherwise, when they have finished spending theirs they just come to us to supply their expenditure desires. (When their money is gone, it is important that we do not supplement it.)

The separation is defined easily this way: spending ideas that come from them come from their money; spending-on-them ideas that come from us cost us. In other words, the next time we hear the words "Can you get me. . . ," "I want a . . . ," or "Would you please buy me. . . ," we know the answer: "If you want that, you can buy it with your own money. If you don't have enough, wait until you have more spending budget. Or, if it's a larger item, put it into your saving budget and start saving." When our kids clearly understand this, and we stick to it, requests decrease.

Note: This rule applies mainly to whims, impulse items, and requests that come when we're out shopping. It's not meant to discourage balanced conversations at home about the things our kids need or would like to have.

To further avoid while-we're-shopping impulse requests, we need to let our kids know before we leave the house what the spending decisions are, including the treat announcement if one is forthcoming. Then we should stick to this plan without change. This demonstrates the following two things to our kids.

a. We are disciplined, we plan our expenditures and follow our plan. (We can't say, "No, it's not what we came for," to them and then buy an impulse item for ourselves. We must be consistent.)

b. They know what to expect or not to expect for themselves. This will make them a lot easier to take shopping. They know what and when and are looking forward to it.

3. We should let our kids spend their spending budget the way they want to, within some broad guidelines. These guidelines are specific to each household, but the basics are usually dietary and content considerations. In other words, we may limit, for example, junk food spending to once a week and establish a no-comic-book rule. But our kids should understand that we aren't trying to control their spending but are helping to guide their diets and guard their minds. We can let our kids know that this is part of spending wisely: spending our money on things Jesus would spend His money on if He were them.

4. Teach your kids the difference between needs, wants, and desires. These three words can be used to help make decisions on whether a certain thing is a wise purchase and also help to decide the level of expense of a purchase. For instance, a snowboard would be defined as a desire.

Clothing is a need, but clothing can range the full gamut from need to desire. Your son may only *need* a pair of jeans that are good quality and fit, but he might *want* a pair of popular, stylish jeans that are a bit more expensive. He probably *desires* the designer jeans that have the name brand, are on the cutting edge of fashion, and are really expensive.

We need to help our kids understand how to find a balance. If the expensive designer jeans are really important to them, they have the money saved, and they are willing to live with no spending money for the rest of the month, we can let them make the purchase.

Getting kids to buy their own basic clothes is not a good budgeting motivator. But we can announce our budget for their clothes and then spend it with their help. We will need to make it clear that when it's gone they will need to buy any extras they want themselves.

Important Note: We live in a society that is style and appearance conscious. We may not agree with the importance placed on this, but for the sake of our kids we sometimes need to follow the phrase, "when in Rome do as the Romans do." Paul said we would be persecuted for our faith, but I don't think being persecuted for our clothing is anything but a hindrance to the Gospel—not to mention what it does to our kids' self-image. We can teach our kids to be wise and moderate without pinching so many pennies that we offend them with the whole process.

5. When shopping with your kids explain the process to them. Show them how to compare prices and quality. Give them the parameters and let them help make the decisions within those parameters.

When we are buying something for them or something that affects them, we can let them know our budgets and our objectives. For example, "We have new tennis shoes in the budget for you this month. My budget is $30.00. My goal is to get you shoes you want by looking for a sale over the next few weeks." Now you've got them involved: they voice their opinions, come up with suggestions, and look for sales. It's important to stay within our original parameters, however, no matter how persuasive they can be.

6. When your children are spending their own money, be sure they go through the wise-buying process. You can walk through it with them and teach them the wise buyers' creed: "Shop till you drop but don't spend till the end." In other words, look and compare and gather information. Pray for wisdom and help in finding the best deal. Then, when you are satisfied your shopping is over, buy it.

7. You mustn't rescue your kids from bad purchases or over-

spending. Teach them how to correct the problem now and in the future, but let them feel the results of their decisions.

8. Also, teach your kids to be responsible for the things they have. Being a good steward doesn't end with a purchase decision. It continues with the proper care of possessions. For example, if your child loses things all the time, you may want to replace an item the first time but explain that the next time it is lost he or she will replace it.

9. If you have children who won't spend and just want to save, you need to help them get beyond this. Be careful not to praise the over-saver for being so frugal. Any imbalance in finances is wrong. You should help the happy hoarder create a spending plan and then see to it they spend it—the same way you would help the over-spender not to go beyond his or her plan.

Activity

Play "shop for a day." Give your kids $15 and tell them to plan and then buy one day's worth of groceries. You should give them shopping lessons. There are some rules.

- They only need to buy the main food items. Condiments, spices, and other things like that can be used from the existing supplies.
- They must provide the ingredients for three sit-down meals.
- The meals must be normal meals your family would eat.
- Fruit, meat, vegetables, breads, and dairy must all be in the day's plans.
- If they have met all the rest of the above requirements, they can buy any dessert they want with the rest of the money.

The idea is to get the children to plan meals wisely and buy wisely. You can play this with 6 to 10 year olds, but you would have to do it with them, asking them questions and leading them through it.

With younger kids it might be more fun to play "see who can get the most treats for a dollar" game.

Pointers

Once you've taught your children how to spend their money wisely, you can help them use the principles behind the spending process for making other decisions.

1. Is this what God wants or am I going after something that's getting my focus and priorities messed up?

2. Does this decision line up with what is right and godly?

3. Will this decision have a positive or negative effect on my future?

DEBT AND CREDIT

Family Motto

"Save and buy, don't buy and borrow; that's how we avoid the sorrow."

Bible Story

You can't take it with you! Unless. . ." (2 Kings 4:1-7).

After reading this story point out that when this man of God died he had debts that could no longer be paid. The result? The creditors were going to take his sons as slaves. Being in debt assumes we know what the future holds—that what it holds will enable us to pay that debt. This man left a negative amount of money when he died so it looks like he took it with him; he spent more than he earned when he was alive.

Perhaps one of the most misunderstood and violated principles in God's Word is credit: borrowing and lending. Many Christians believe you should never borrow money. In fact, they go to God's Word and try to pick individual Scripture verses that would lend themselves to that interpretation. Others operate no differently than the world: not only do they borrow, they borrow in excess.

God does not prohibit using credit; He simply lays down very clear guidelines for how credit should be used. There are three basic principles: credit should never be normal for God's people; credit should never be long-term; never sign surety (taking on an obligation to pay without an absolutely certain way to pay).

When teaching your kids keep the rule and the exception to the rule in the correct order. The rule is "Stay out of debt." There are a few exceptions, but if we keep focused on and plan according to the rule we'll be better prepared to keep the exceptions out of our lives.

Faith Story
Tell a family horror. . .uh, that's a family *borrow* story.

Memory Verse
"The rich rule over the poor, and the borrower is servant to the lender" (Proverbs 22:7).

Definitions
Debt is spending money we don't have. "Debt then payments" is actually "saving then purchasing" in reverse. With debt, we get something and then start saving for it. But instead of putting the money in the bank to earn interest as we save, now we're being charged interest for borrowing it.

When we save with a plan to purchase, God stays in charge. When we "buy now, pay later" we've committed money we haven't earned or saved yet. Or, more importantly, we've committed money that God hasn't given us yet or shown us what to do with. How can we be good stewards when we are running ahead of the Master? God's plan is for us to learn "delayed gratification," which is a fancy way of saying we need to learn to wait until we've saved the money for something before we buy it.

Credit is used when someone is willing to trust us to buy now and pay later. If we have a credit card, the credit card company will let us buy something now (without actually paying for it) and they will send us a bill for it at the end of the month.

We can use credit without getting into debt. If we plan our spending, save for the things we want and desire, shop properly and then buy with a credit card, we will be able to pay for it when the bill comes. This way we have the use of credit without the interest charges and without spending money that God hasn't given us yet.

Creditors ask three main questions before lending money: Are you reliable? Is your income large enough to afford the payments? Is your income steady and secure enough for you to keep making your payments? The funny thing about these questions is that they boil down to one: The bank wants to know, "If you budgeted and saved, could you buy it yourself?"

Tips

1. We recommend allowing kids to get a credit card and teaching them how to use it. (At the earliest, this should happen after they have been using the teen budget for some time and are handling all the elements well.) We should establish and discuss some rules before going ahead with this. If we and our kids agree on the rules ahead of time (even to the point of writing them down) then they will understand when we enforce those rules. It's important not to soften the rule c (below).

    a. Use the credit card only for budgeted items.

    b. Pay it off at the end of every month.

    c. Cut it up the first time it's not paid off on time.

2. We should help our kids understand debt from a stewardship point of view. We don't want to just leave them with the rule. We want to go beyond it to the reason and the Ruler.

3. When we borrow, we are committing ourselves to something that we don't know we can keep. Who knows what the future

holds? When we save, we are acting on what we think, what we intend to do, and we are leaving room for God to change it. If we trust God and don't have the money for something we want, we won't borrow; we'll take it as a sign that God doesn't want us to get that thing. God might have a different and better idea for us.

4. There are some other practical reasons not to borrow that we tell our kids.

- The average American family pays $7,000 a year in interest. With earning power, over ten years that's $150,000. Imagine what that means over a lifetime!

- The Bible says the borrower is servant to the lender. If we are stewards, we should only have one master. When we have debts we are tied down to obligations that may limit what God can give us to do.

- God advises us to stay out of debt because He loves us and wants the best for us.

5. Teach your kids to build their finances a little at a time and to be encouraged by steady growth. So there will be no surprises, let them know when they're young that you will not cosign for a loan for them. (Unfortunately, it's usually a parent giving in to a cosigning request that plunges young adults into lives of debt.) If you teach your kids to plan ahead, save, and spend wisely within their budget and means, they shouldn't get to that point. If they do face this problem, help them find another way.

Don't give in to something that will strap your children's finances and get them into a bad habit of using credit. If it's something urgent or very important, pray about it. God may want you to give it to them. (If you don't have the ability to give them the cash, then don't consider cosigning. That would be against God's principles.)

6. Caution your kids about lending money to their friends, because if they follow God's financial principles when they are young, as adults they will have great credit, assets, and savings—

and no debt. That will make them ideal candidates to be asked for help by those in financial trouble. Teach them the following principles about lending.

- They should be willing to lend and/or give without expecting anything in return. Prayer is necessary; sometimes the answer to whether they should lend the money may be "no." This could be either because they are unable to or because their friends need to face the consequences of bad decisions. Our kids should be ready to help counsel others in what the Bible says about money management. One time God may want them just to give, another time to lend.

- A Christian brother or family member should never be charged interest.

- When they lend, they should count the money as given and never worry about it again. This means when they lend they should be able to afford giving the amount as a gift.

- They should never cosign. (The only possible exception to this is if they have the money and can afford to pay off loans if their friends default. In that case they might as well just lend it. Or give it.)

Activity
War on debt

1. Make a family scrapbook. Get everyone in the family involved. After reading the Bible story, going over the memory verse, and reading the definition to your family, have an open discussion about debt and credit. Have a large inexpensive scrapbook and all the usual stuff at hand (pens, old magazines, newspapers, photocopies of pages in this book that contain debt and credit information and statistics, glue, felt pens). Title your scrapbook, "War on Debt." The following are some ideas for the contents of the scrapbook.

- Bible verses on debt written out under "What the Bible Says." Some sample verses you can use: Psalm 37:21; Proverbs 22:7; Luke 6:34-35; Romans 13:8.
- Newspaper articles on debt.
- Quotes and photocopies from this book.
- Magazine and newspaper ads compelling people to purchase with debt.
- Articles about the national debt, bankruptcies, and any other debt-related items.
- A written interview by one of your kids with you (or someone else they know) telling a faith story about debt.
- At the end of the book, title a page "Soldiers Against Debt" and have everyone in the family sign it. Perhaps a family picture can be glued in. This is your debt army.
- Continue to collect and fill the scrapbook.

Offer a cash prize for the family member who finds the best scrapbook contribution for the week. This may seem like a lot of work, but your kids will have fun, they'll begin to learn and internalize the information and, most importantly, they'll never forget it.

2. Also, you can play *Larry Burkett's Money Matters™* (board game), *The Christian Financial Concepts™ Game!* This game is an ideal way to get discussions going on financial topics. And your family will have fun while they learn the following:

- Stewardship
- It's not how much money you have but how you manage it that makes the difference.
- Get out of debt.
- Stay out of debt.
- Saving
- Giving
- Budgeting

Pointers

People who live God's way—in the plus and building, in the black and saving—prepare themselves to help and give to others. People who continue to spend all they have and go into debt consume their resources and continually look for more. These people cannot be givers because everything is spent on themselves.

The principles behind debt and credit management help us teach our kids to get their eyes off themselves and onto God, the Gospel, and others. The activity for this principle is very important, because as we instill a commitment to surplus rather than debt management, we are instilling in our children the ability to make decisions that consider others rather than just themselves.

Teaching this principle in this hands-on financial area gives us the opportunity, as parents, to turn our kids into givers instead of takers focused on themselves—givers in friendships, givers in their marriage, givers to their children, givers to their church, givers to their employer, givers to their community, (and givers to their parents when we're older.)

Also, the balance taught here between being generous with available resources and using God's wisdom and guidance can be applied to all of these other areas, preventing our adult children from giving more than they should and burning out. (Another name for burnout is time and energy debt.)

CONCLUSION

We have covered twelve principles and provided practical ways of teaching them. We suggest focusing on one a month. This would take a year to deal with the whole course of teaching. This would establish these principles as foundations on which to build. The training can, of course, be repeated the next year as the kids grow older, building on the knowledge already gained.

Financial parenting can help us prepare our children, grounded in God's basic principles, for every area of their lives and for the rest of their lives. *"Train a child in the way he should go, and when he is old he will not turn from it"* (Proverbs 22:6).

We want to add to what we said earlier about this Scripture. Since the book of Proverbs is not a book of laws or promises but a book of principles, our action plan coming out of this verse must correspond to a principle. If it were a law, we could have it enforced. If it were a promise, we would expect fulfillment from the Promise Maker. But since it is a principle we must look to the process behind the principle, or the action plan it subscribes to, for the mentioned result.

The process or action plan is *"Train a child in the way he should go."* The way we do that is spelled out over and over again in God's Word. We need to teach our children what the Bible says and help them apply it to their lives and live it out.

We trust this section has helped you and given you practical ideas and information that will aid you in the process. We would like to conclude this book with some very important information about our generation of kids.

Wrap-up

The Call to Arms

"*esus went through all the towns and villages, teaching in their synagogues, preaching the good news of the kingdom and healing every disease and sickness. When he saw the crowds, he had compassion on them, because they were harassed and helpless, like sheep without a shepherd. Then he said to his disciples, 'The harvest is plentiful but the workers are few. Ask the Lord of the harvest, therefore, to send out workers into his harvest field'"* (Matthew 9:35-38).

Was Jesus making a general statement about the people of the Earth and how they would be during the New Testament era when He said, "*The harvest is plentiful*"? We believe that may have been part of it, but look at what verse 36 says. "*When he saw the crowds, he had compassion on them, because **they were harassed and helpless, like sheep without a shepherd**. Then he said to his disciples, 'The harvest is plenti-*

ful but the workers are few'" (emphasis added). He was specifically moved by the crowds He was ministering to and their spiritual state.

Not long after this the New Testament church started with a bang, with thousands of people responding to the news of Jesus and what He had done. Eventually the book of Acts records that those people turned the world upside down.

God had prepared the world for Jesus' timely arrival. The Greek language was an international language and everyone in the known world was supposed to speak it. The domination of the Roman Empire had brought peace over large areas of land, which made for ease of travel and trade. Roman roads and shipping routes also made travel a lot easier than at other times in history. God sent Jesus at the right time. He prepared everything for the establishing of His church and the evangelizing of the known world.

But God didn't just prepare communication and transportation. He prepared people's hearts.

The Roman Empire was in the Age of the Entertainer. During Jesus' time Jerusalem was at its zenith of architecture and culture. Herod the Great had rebuilt the temple. He also had built a palace, a fortress, and, for entertainment, a large theater and a stadium. Rome was in decline while Jesus ministered in its empire.

There are two things prominent in the last age of an empire: a hopeless eat-drink-and-be-merry-for-tomorrow-we-die attitude and a spiritual renewal. Jesus knew where the world was in its stages. He prophesied the destruction of Jerusalem in A.D. 70. When He looked on the people He knew they were without hope: *"harassed and helpless, like sheep without a shepherd."* He knew they were ready for spiritual renewal, the moving of God's Spirit, and the establishing of the New Testament church. *"The harvest is plentiful."*

God appointed this time in the decline of the Roman Empire

because, like the prodigal son, a nation, an empire, a generation of people must reach the end of their strength and hope before they are ready to look up. God had not only prepared the time, the earth, the communication, and the transportation, He had prepared the hearts of a generation.

Where are we today? What is in the hearts of a generation that is just entering the work force and a generation that is being brought up in this time? As we established earlier, America is in the same stage of an empire as Rome was in Jesus' day: the last stage of decline, the Age of the Entertainer.

The generation that is growing up right now absolutely parallels the generation Jesus was looking at when He observed the crowd as being *"harassed and helpless, like sheep without a shepherd."* The stage of world history we are in today matches the one of Jesus' day. And the state of the hearts of this generation matches the state of the people's hearts Jesus saw and on whom He had compassion.

Today, in our society and in the church, people are beginning to sound the alarm.

- Eighty-five percent of people who accept Jesus as Savior do so before the age of 18.
- By the year 2000, over 50 percent of the world's population will be under the age of 18.

It doesn't take a genius to see where we should be spending our time. We should be spending it on a huge generation that is growing up in the same stage of an empire as in Jesus' time, on people with the same spiritual condition Jesus identified as *"harassed and helpless, like sheep without a shepherd."* Yet only 30 percent of church-going youth in North America have taken ownership of their faith by the time they graduate from high school.

Our intent is not to discourage but to encourage. God is working and preparing the hearts of a segment of this generation. While this generation, in this age of history, is coming to the place where they have nowhere to look but up to God, simultaneously God is preparing a generation of youth that will be raised and ready. He is preparing the hearts of kids to reach out to their peers, to "generation X."

To set the stage for what He will do next, we as Christian parents and leaders need to prepare for the harvest because, once again, it is plentiful. We need to work with our children and youth and prepare them as leaders for the next generation. If their lives are grounded in biblical truths, they won't be carried away like their peers. They will be ready to reap the harvest.

Does this mean we must raise all our kids to be missionaries, pastors, and evangelists? No! It means we need to raise them as sons and daughters of God who understand and live by God's principles.

We need to form them into a group that can reach out and offer hope to a generation without hope. They will be able to do this because their lives will be founded in and on the eternal principles of God rather than the passing fancies of progressive generational thought.

The current financial I.Q. of our children only reflects their spiritual state—just as the prodigal son's spending habits demonstrated his heart. Let us not pound on the anvil of financial education. Let's work on the root and use the topic of finances to point our children to God and establish their lives on His principles.

This is a call to arms! It's a call to call our children into God's arms!

Jesus said, *"I will show you what he is like who comes to me and hears my words and puts them into practice. He is like a man building a house, who dug down deep and laid the foundation on rock. When a flood came, the torrent struck that house but could not shake it, because it was well built. But the one who hears my words and does not put them into practice is like a man who built a house on the ground without a foundation. The moment the torrent struck that house, it collapsed and its destruction was complete"* (Luke 6:47-49).

APPENDIX

Books (see also the following resource lists from CFC and from Lightwave)

Budget Workbook for College Students (untitled curriculum), Larry Burkett with Todd Temple (Christian Financial Concepts) (**publication date 1997**).

Every Child Can Succeed, Cynthia Ulrich Tobias (Focus on the Family).

Fast Cash for Kids, Bonnie Drew (Career Press).

Get a Grip on Your Money (for ages 16 to 21), Larry Burkett (Christian Financial Concepts).

Mom, Can I Have That?: Dr. Tightwad Answers Your Kids' Questions About Money, Janet Bodnar (Kiplinger/Times).

A Money Book for Ages 11 to 14 (untitled curriculum), Larry Burkett with Todd Temple (Christian Financial Concepts) (**publication date 1997**).

A Money Book for Ages 15 to 18 (untitled curriculum), Larry Burkett with Todd Temple (Christian Financial Concepts) (**publication date 1997**).

Money Skills: 101 Activities to Teach Your Child About Money, Bonnie Drew (Career Press).

Money-Smart Kids (and Parents Too!), Janet Bodnar (Kiplinger/Times).

105 Questions Children Ask About Money, Rick Osborne, et al. (Tyndale House) (**publication date 1997**).

A Penny Saved: Teaching Your Children the Values and Life Skills They Will Need to Live in the Real World, Neale S. Godfrey (Simon & Schuster).

Piggy Bank to Credit Card, Linda Barbanel (Crown Publishers).

Raising Money-Wise Kids, Judith Briles (Northfield/Moody Press).

Strong-Willed Child or Dreamer? Dr. Ron L. Braund and Dr. Dana Scott Spears (Thomas Nelson).

Surviving the Money Jungle: A Junior High Study in Handling Money, Larry Burkett (Christian Financial Concepts).

Teach Your Child the Value of Money, Harold and Sandy Moe (Harsand Press).

365 Ways to Help Your Child Learn to Achieve, Cheri Fuller (Piñon).

The Way They Learn, Cynthia Ulrich Tobias (Focus on the Family).

Newsletters and magazines

Focus on the Family (1-800-661-9800) offers the following magazines:

- *Clubhouse Jr.* (fun crafts, games, and more—all emphasizing scriptural principles for ages 4 to 8)

- *Clubhouse* (puzzles and faith-building stories for ages 8 to 12)

- *Brio* (from fashion and food to fitness and faith for teen girls)

- *Breakaway* (gives the low down on sports, celebrities, girls and also advice, humor, and spiritual guidance for teen boys).

Grace Parenting Newsletter, available through Lightwave Publishing.

Lightwave Kids Club Magazine, available through Lightwave Publishing (carries "Larry the Cat" aka Larry Burkett article each issue).

Money Matters for Kids Newsletter (featuring Larry the Cat), available through Christian Financial Concepts (periodically published as an added benefit to subscribers of CFC's *Money Matters* newsletter).

Games and Bank

Larry Burkett's Money Matters™, The Christian Financial Concepts™ Game! for ages 7 to adult (ChariotVictor Publishing).

Money Wise Kids: Practice money management and hone math and value skills (Home School Warehouse).

Sticky Situations: The McGee and Me Board Game (Tyndale) (available from Lightwave Publishing).

My Giving Bank (ChariotVictor Publishing).

RESOURCES FOR THE WHOLE FAMILY
AVAILABLE FROM YOUR LOCAL CHRISTIAN BOOKSTORE OR
FROM CHRISTIAN FINANCIAL CONCEPTS
(All items are books unless otherwise specified.)

Answers to Your Family's Financial Questions, Larry Burkett (Focus on the Family).

Business by the Book, Larry Burkett (Thomas Nelson).

The Complete Financial Guide for Young Couples, Larry Burkett (Victor Books).

Debt-Free Living (book—also available on tape), Larry Burkett (Moody Press).

The Financial Freedom Video Library Series: (3 videos) Managing

Possessions; Using Resources Wisely; Personal Finances (ideal for Sunday school and small groups, each video is divided into two segments for maximum flexibility of presentation), Larry Burkett (Moody Press).

The Financial Planning Organizer, Complete Edition (workbook, workshop audio tapes, CFC Will Kit, all in a binder), Larry Burkett (CFC).

The Financial Planning Workshop, A family budgeting seminar (Financial Planning Workbook may be purchased separately—also available in video or audio series), Larry Burkett (CFC).

Finding the Career That Fits You, Lee Ellis and Larry Burkett (Moody Press).

How to Manage Your Money: An in-depth Bible study on personal finances, (workbook—also available in video or audio series with instructor's manual), Larry Burkett.

Investing for the Future, Larry Burkett (Victor Books).

Money Before Marriage (a book for engaged couples—includes personality analysis), Larry Burkett and Michael E. Taylor (Moody Press).

Money Matters, a Christian economic newsletter (CFC).

Money Smart: Insights into Your Finances, Larry Burkett (Moody Press).

105 Questions Kids Ask About Money, Rick Osborne, et al (Tyndale) **(publication date late 1996)**.

The PathFinder (Personality Analysis), Lee Ellis (Career Pathways, a ministry of CFC).

Saving Money Any Way You Can: How to Become a Frugal Family,

Mike Yorkey (Servant Publications).

Smart Money: Understanding and Successfully Controlling Your Financial Behavior, Jerry and Ramona Tuma (Multnomah).

The Word on Finances: Topical Scriptures and Commentary, Larry Burkett (Moody Press).

Using Your Money Wisely: Biblical Principles Under Scrutiny, Larry Burkett (Moody Press).

Women Leaving the Workplace: How to Make the Transition from Work to Home, Larry Burkett (Moody Press).

Your Career in Changing Times, Lee Ellis and Larry Burkett (Moody Press).

Your Finances in Changing Times, Larry Burkett (Moody Press).

For a complete list of resources available from CFC or a subscription to the *Money Matters* Christian economic newsletter, call 1-800-772-1976, fax (770) 536-7226, visit our Internet site (shown below), or write to the following address.

Christian Financial Concepts
PO Box 2377
Gainesville, GA 30503-2377
Internet address: http://www.cfcministry.org

**RESOURCES TO TEACH YOUR CHILDREN ABOUT
GOD AND THE BIBLE AVAILABLE FROM YOUR LOCAL
CHRISTIAN BOOKSTORE OR FROM LIGHTWAVE PUBLISHING**
(All items are books unless otherwise specified.)

Adventure Bible Handbook: A Wild and Spectacular High-Tech Trip Through the Bible (Zondervan: Grand Rapids).

Adventure Bible Handbook, CD-Rom Game (Zondervan: Grand Rapids).

Grace Parenting Newsletter, giving tips and aids to help parents pass on their faith to their children.

Larry Burkett's Money Matters™, The Christian Financial Concepts™ Game! for ages 7 to adult (ChariotVictor Publishing).

Lightwave Kid's Club Magazine.

LWTV Videos, available through Lightwave Publishing.

101 Questions Children Ask About God, Rick Osborne, et al. (Tyndale).

102 Questions Children Ask About the Bible, Rick Osborne, et al. (Tyndale).

103 Questions Children Ask About Right from Wrong, Rick Osborne, et al. (Tyndale).

104 Questions Children Ask About Heaven and Angels, Rick Osborne, et al. (Tyndale).

105 Questions Children Ask About Money, Rick Osborne, et al. (Tyndale) (**publication date late 1996**).

The Singing Bible, Elaine Osborne (4 cassettes) (Word Publishing).

Sticky Situations: The McGee and Me Board Game (Tyndale).

For a complete list of resources available from Lightwave or to receive the *Grace Parenting Newsletter,* please call 1-800-555-9881 and ask for an information pack or write to:

Lightwave Publishing
PO Box 160
Maple Ridge, B.C.
Canada V2X7G1

Lightwave Publishing
33, 800-5th Ave Ste 101
Seattle, WA 98104-3191

Internet address: http://www.beacom.com/lw

ORGANIZATIONS TO HELP YOU

BANK CARD HOLDERS OF AMERICA
(referral service and information about low interest/no annual fee
and secured credit cards)
560 Herndon Pkwy Ste 120
Herndon VA 22070
(703) 481-1110

CHRISTIAN FAMILIES TODAY
Greg and Connie Brezina
200 Providence Rd
Fayetteville GA 30214-2844

COMPASSION INTERNATIONAL
(offers a child sponsorship program)
3955 Cragwood Dr
Colorado Springs CO 80933

CONSUMER CREDIT COUNSELING SERVICE
8611 Second Ave Ste 100
Silver Spring MD 10910
(800) 388-2227

CONSUMER FRESH START
601 Pennsylvania Ave NW Ste 900
Washington DC 20004
(800) 933-2372

FOCUS ON THE FAMILY
Colorado Springs CO 80995
(719) 531-3400 (800) A FAMILY

GREGG AND SONO HARRIS
(Home Schooling Information)
182 SE Kane Rd
Gresham OR 97030
(800) 775-5422

JOSH MC DOWELL MINISTRY
Box 1000
Dallas TX 75221
(214) 234-0645

THE MOORE FOUNDATION
Raymond and Dorothy Moore
Box 1
Camas WA 98607

THE NATIONAL FOUNDATION FOR CONSUMER CREDIT
8611 Second Ave Ste 100
Silver Spring MD 10910
(800) 388-2227

Christian
Financial
Concepts

A CFC | Recommended Children's Resource

Larry Burkett, founder and president of Christian Financial Concepts, is the best-selling author of 49 books on business and personal finances and two novels. He also hosts two radio programs broadcast on hundreds of stations worldwide.

Larry earned B.S. degrees in marketing and in finance, and recently an Honorary Doctorate in Economics was conferred by Southwest Baptist University. For several years he served as a manager in the space program at Cape Canaveral, Florida. He also has been vice president of an electronics manufacturing firm. Larry's education, business experience, and solid understanding of God's Word enable him to give practical, Bible-based financial counsel to families, churches, and businesses.

Founded in 1976, Christian Financial Concepts, Inc. is a nonprofit, nondenominational ministry dedicated to helping God's people gain a clear understanding of how to manage their money according to scriptural principles. Although practical assistance is provided on many levels, the purpose of CFC is simply *to bring glory to God by freeing His people from financial bondage so they may serve Him to their utmost.*

One major avenue of ministry involves the training of volunteers in budget and debt counseling and linking them with financially troubled families and individuals through a nationwide referral network. CFC also provides financial management seminars and workshops for churches and other groups. (Formats available include audio, video, and live instruction.) A full line of printed and audio-visual materials related to money management is available through CFC's materials department (1-800-722-1976) or via the Internet (http://www.cfcministry.org).

Career Pathways, another outreach of Christian Financial Concepts, helps teenagers and adults find their occupational calling. The Career Pathways "assessment" gauges a person's work priorities, skills, vocational interests, and personality. Reports in each of these areas define a person's strengths, weaknesses, and unique, God-given pattern for work.

Visit CFC's Internet site at http://www.cfcministry.org or write to the address below for further information.

Christian Financial Concepts
PO Box 2458
Gainesville GA 30503-2458

L I G H T *wave*

Rick Osborne, author and speaker, encourages and teaches parents to pass on their faith to their children. He is the founder and president of Lightwave Publishing and Lightwave Kids Club.

For the past twelve years Rick and his wife Elaine have been developing and producing high quality materials that help parents teach their children about God and the Bible. Among the 30 books and resources are *101 Questions Children Ask About God, The Singing Bible, Adventure Bible Handbook,* and *Lightwave Kids Club Magazine.* Rick and Elaine have been featured on a number of Christian television and radio programs. They reside in British Columbia with their three children.

Lightwave's mission is to encourage, assist, and equip parents to pass on their Christian faith to their children. Lightwave, together with Bible publishers Zondervan, Word, and Tyndale House, has been successfully producing high quality children's books, music and games for over 10 years.

Lightwave's learning resources have been sold or endorsed by such ministries as Josh McDowell Ministries, Campus Crusade for Christ, Christian Financial Concepts, the 700 Club, Living Way Ministries, The Christian Research Institute, The Full Gospel Businessmen's Fellowship, and the American Family Association.

Visit Lightwave's Internet site at www.beacom.com/lw or write to the address below for further information.

Lightwave Publishing Inc.
800 5th Ave Ste 101
Seattle WA 98104-3191
or
Lightwave Publishing Inc.
Box 160
Maple Ridge, B.C. CANADA V2X 7G1

ChariotVICTOR
PUBLISHING
A DIVISION OF COOK COMMUNICATIONS

ChariotVictor Publishing assists the spiritual development of believers by publishing products which foster saving faith, increase understanding of the Bible, and help apply Christian values to everyday life through:
• Chariot Books
(for children and youth)
• Victor Books
(for Christian living)
• Lion Books
(for seekers)
• Rainfall Educational Toys and Games
(for the entire family)

When you are looking for fun ways to bring the Bible to life in the lives of your family, look to ChariotVictor Publishing.

ChariotVictor Publishing has hundreds of books, toys, games, and videos that help teach your children the Bible and apply it to their everyday lives. Look for these educational, inspirational, and fun products at your local Christian bookstore.